Beyond the Good Friday Agreement

2018 marks the 20th anniversary of the Good Friday Agreement. When it was signed few would have imagined Brexit. This book examines the impact of the Good Friday Agreement on internal and cross-border political and economic cooperation between Northern Ireland, Ireland and Britain, in the context of Brexit. It also examines the impact of Brexit to date and concludes with some scenarios about the longer-term impact of Brexit on the Good Friday Agreement itself and on Northern Ireland's constitutional status.

The volume comprises chapters from leading academics in the fields of Northern Irish and comparative politics who deal with economic and political aspects of the Good Friday Agreement, making an original contribution to the current debates on conflict resolution. It provides a theoretical framework by renowned expert on consociationalism, Brendan O'Leary, as well as a chapter on the British–Irish relationship in the 21st century by renowned Northern Ireland specialist John Coakley.

This book was originally published as a special issue of *Ethnopolitics*.

Etain Tannam is Associate Professor of International Peace Studies at Trinity College Dublin, Ireland.

Beyond the Good Friday Agreement

In the Midst of Brexit

Edited by
Etain Tannam

Routledge
Taylor & Francis Group

LONDON AND NEW YORK

First published 2019
by Routledge
2 Park Square, Milton Park, Abingdon, Oxon, OX14 4RN, UK

and by Routledge
52 Vanderbilt Avenue, New York, NY 10017, USA

First issued in paperback 2020

Routledge is an imprint of the Taylor & Francis Group, an informa business

British Library Cataloguing-in-Publication Data
A catalogue record for this book is available from the British Library

ISBN 13: 978-0-367-58537-2 (pbk)
ISBN 13: 978-1-138-38547-4 (hbk)

Typeset in Times New Roman
by codeMantra

Publisher's Note
The publisher accepts responsibility for any inconsistencies that may have arisen during the conversion of this book from journal articles to book chapters, namely the possible inclusion of journal terminology.

Disclaimer
Every effort has been made to contact copyright holders for their permission to reprint material in this book. The publishers would be grateful to hear from any copyright holder who is not here acknowledged and will undertake to rectify any errors or omissions in future editions of this book.

Contents

Citation Information   vi
Notes on Contributors   viii

1 The Twilight of the United Kingdom & *Tiocfaidh ár lá*:
   Twenty Years after the Good Friday Agreement
   Brendan O'Leary   1

2 Intergovernmental and Cross-Border Civil Service
   Cooperation: The Good Friday Agreement and Brexit
   Etain Tannam   21

3 The Irish–Northern Irish Economic Relationship: The Belfast
   Agreement, UK Devolution and the EU
   John Bradley   41

4 The EU's Influence on the Peace Process and Agreement
   in Northern Ireland in Light of Brexit
   Katy Hayward and Mary C. Murphy   54

5 Brexit, Bordering and Bodies on the Island of Ireland
   Cathal McCall   70

6 The British–Irish Relationship in the Twenty-first Century
   John Coakley   84

7 Postscript: New British Questions or *2019 And All That!*
   Brendan O'Leary   103

Index   113

Citation Information

The chapters in this book were originally published in the journal *Ethnopolitics*, volume 17, issue 3 (June 2018). When citing this material, please use the original page numbering for each article, as follows:

Chapter 1
The Twilight of the United Kingdom & Tiocfaidh ár lá: *Twenty Years after the Good Friday Agreement*
Brendan O'Leary
Ethnopolitics, volume 17, issue 3 (June 2018) pp. 223–242

Chapter 2
Intergovernmental and Cross-Border Civil Service Cooperation: The Good Friday Agreement and Brexit
Etain Tannam
Ethnopolitics, volume 17, issue 3 (June 2018) pp. 243–262

Chapter 3
The Irish–Northern Irish Economic Relationship: The Belfast Agreement, UK Devolution and the EU
John Bradley
Ethnopolitics, volume 17, issue 3 (June 2018) pp. 263–275

Chapter 4
The EU's Influence on the Peace Process and Agreement in Northern Ireland in Light of Brexit
Katy Hayward and Mary C. Murphy
Ethnopolitics, volume 17, issue 3 (June 2018) pp. 276–291

Chapter 5
Brexit, Bordering and Bodies on the Island of Ireland
Cathal McCall
Ethnopolitics, volume 17, issue 3 (June 2018) pp. 292–305

Chapter 6
The British–Irish Relationship in the Twenty-first Century
John Coakley
Ethnopolitics, volume 17, issue 3 (June 2018) pp. 306–324

Chapter 7

Postscript: New British Questions or 2019 And All That!
Brendan O'Leary
Ethnopolitics, volume 17, issue 3 (June 2018) pp. 325–333

For any permission-related enquiries please visit:
http://www.tandfonline.com/page/help/permissions

Notes on Contributors

John Bradley is Research Professor at the Economic and Social Research Institute, Ireland.

John Coakley is Distinguished International Professor at Queen's University Belfast, UK and an Emeritus Professor at University College Dublin, Ireland.

Katy Hayward is Reader in the School of Social Sciences, Education and Social Work at Queen's University Belfast, UK.

Cathal McCall is Professor in the School of History, Anthropology, Philosophy and Politics at Queen's University Belfast, UK. He is also affiliated with The Senator George J. Mitchell Institute for Global Peace, Security and Justice at Queen's University Belfast, UK.

Mary C. Murphy holds a Jean Monnet Chair in European Integration and is Lecturer in Politics in the Department of Government and Politics at University College Cork, Ireland.

Brendan O'Leary is Lauder Professor of Political Science at the Perelman Center for Political Science & Economics at the University of Pennsylvania, Philadelphia, USA.

Etain Tannam is Associate Professor of International Peace Studies at Trinity College Dublin, Ireland.

The Twilight of the United Kingdom & *Tiocfaidh ár lá*: Twenty Years after the Good Friday Agreement

BRENDAN O'LEARY

ABSTRACT   The Good Friday or Belfast Agreement was reached just over 20 years ago. This article introduces a special issue devoted to appraising its subsequent trajectory. It provides a brief resumé of the Agreement's contents as a peace agreement, and as a regional consociation with confederal and federal possibilities. The outworkings and partial implementation of the Agreement are reviewed against a theoretical appraisal of the circumstances under which consociations decay, organically dissolve, or definitively break down. Northern Ireland is not in these circumstances, yet. The impact of UK's referendum to leave the European Union (EU) is evaluated as well as 'the year of the four votes' in 2016–2017, which have jointly left Northern Ireland without a functioning executive or Assembly, and politically divided over the minority UK Conservative government's plans to give effect to the referendum result—Northern Ireland voted to remain in the EU, and contrary to some suggestions, joint membership of the EU by the UK and Ireland was integral to the making and design of the 1998 Agreement. Future scenarios are sketched.

Anniversaries are occasions for celebrations or commemorations or both. In 2018 the Good Friday Agreement, also known as the Belfast Agreement, is 20 years old.[1] Currently, it is unknown whether it is to be placed in formaldehyde, renewed with or without significant emendation, or about to die. The Agreement is a consociational text and a peace agreement with federal and consociational characteristics. It sought to resolve a conflict that in its most recent manifestation flowed from the control regime exercised by the UUP (Ulster Unionist Party) that had lasted from the British creation of Northern Ireland until 1972. That regime had been politically, nationally, ethnically, culturally, religiously, and economically discriminatory, disorganizing the cultural Catholic population, largely of Irish native descent, and organizing the cultural Protestants who were largely of British settler descent (O'Leary, 2019a, 2019b).

Finalized in Stormont Castle Buildings on 10 April 1998, the Agreement was endorsed by 8 of the 10 parties that had won seats in elections to the Northern Ireland Peace Forum in

1996, and subsequently was ratified by the citizens of both parts of Ireland in concurrent referendums held on 22 May 1998, endorsed by 94% of those who voted in Ireland, and by 71% of those who voted in Northern Ireland.[2] Ireland and the UK pledged to be the guarantors in an international treaty.[3] 'The Agreement,' unless otherwise specified, refers here to the text finalized at the multi-party negotiations chaired by US Senator George C Mitchell and his colleagues, and distributed to all households in Northern Ireland;[4] the UK legislative enactment of the provisions regarding the internal government of Northern Ireland;[5] and to the respective legislative enactments of the treaty by the two sovereign governments.

If the Agreement dies in the near future it will have lasted longer than the average written constitution of a sovereign state (Elkins, Ginsburg, & Melton, 2009). Reasonable observers —and there are some—would have to code it as a partial success because it has played a major role in consolidating the end of significant ethno-national violence and counter-insurgency operations; in facilitating the reform of policing and judicial institutions; in embedding equality and anti-discrimination law; and in eventually opening a decade of continuous if contentious power-sharing between the Democratic Unionist Party (DUP) and Sinn Féin (O'Leary, 2019c).[6]

As the Agreement's third decade begins, it is equally possible, however, that three of its key institutions—the Northern Ireland Assembly and Executive, and the North-South Ministerial Council—will go into suspended animation, officially or otherwise. If that happens, they are not likely to re-emerge until after the UK's exit from the European Union (EU), which has been fitfully, and chaotically, underway since the summer of 2016, or, until the DUP's 'supply and confidence' agreement with the minority Conservative government, in existence since the summer of 2017, comes to an end.[7] Current negotiations suggest that UKEXIT from the EU will begin in January 2021, following the EU–UK agreement to accept a transition until December 2020 during which the UK will remain governed by EU law but not participate within EU institutions.[8] The third possibility would lead to the renewal and emendation of the Agreement: there is a case for some minimal changes, consistent with the Agreement's own provisions for review and amendment, following arguments anticipated elsewhere (McCrudden, McGarry, O'Leary, & Schwartz, 2016), and there will have to be some amendments because of UKEXIT.

The Content: Consociation Plus

Strand One of the multi-party and intergovernmental negotiations produced internal consociational arrangements for Northern Ireland (O'Leary, 1999). A cross-party, cross-national, cross-community power-sharing executive was established in Belfast, based on a dual premiership—two first ministers differ only in their titles, and not in their powers—and a cabinet formed through the d'Hondt allocation rule (McEvoy, 2015; O'Leary, Grofman, & Elklit, 2005). Proportionality rules determine executive formation (d'Hondt), the electoral system used to return the Assembly (STV-PR), the Assembly's committee structure (d'Hondt), and the restructured Northern Ireland Police Service and Policing Board (Doyle, 2010; McGarry & O'Leary, 2004). Cultural autonomy had earlier been placed on an equal footing in one key domain in 1992: all schooling systems are equally and proportionally funded (Fontana, 2017). The two sovereign governments pledged to govern with rigorous impartiality regarding rights, religion, and culture, whether Northern Ireland remained within the UK, or reunified with Ireland.

The Agreement contained multiple veto-provisions to prevent simple majoritarian dominance. Cross-community consent legislative rules in the Assembly require *either* concurrent majorities of registered unionists and nationalists for the passage of laws ('parallel consent') *or* a qualified majority of at least 60%, including at least 40% of registered nationalists and unionists, respectively ('weighted majority'). These rules may be triggered by a petition of concern, signed by 30 Members of the Legislative Assembly (MLAs).[9] A two-thirds resolution among all MLAs may trigger an extraordinary general election before the Assembly's statutory four-year term expires. This rule was agreed in preference to a proposal that the UK Secretary of State should have the power to dissolve or suspend the Assembly—a sign of the local parties' commitment to their self-government. Subsequently, to suspend the Assembly in February 2000, the UK Secretary of State, Peter Mandelson, had to pass fresh primary legislation, the Northern Ireland Act 2000, through the Westminster parliament, and outside the remit of the Agreement, but the Suspension Act was repealed as part of the making of the St Andrews Agreement in 2006—and had never been recognized by Ireland's government.

The Agreement was not just consociational, however (McGarry & O'Leary, 2006a; 2006b; O'Leary, 1999), and departed from Arend Lijphart's prescriptions in important respects; e.g. the Northern Assembly does not use list-PR for elections but rather STV-PR, and was designed to operate within overarching confederal and federalizing arrangements (or at least possibilities). The external dimensions of the Agreement, flowing from Strands Two and Three of the negotiations, produced the North-South Ministerial Council, the British-Irish Council, and the British-Irish Intergovernmental Conference. The Agreement was made with, and by, the leaders of national, and not just ethnic or religious communities; majorities in two simultaneous and separate referendums in different polities endorsed it; and it was the first consociation endorsed in concurrent referendums in different states. There were prospects of shared authority in the oversight arrangements agreed between the patron states, though these have since been downplayed. A novel model of 'double protection' was sketched, though it remains to be fully implemented: upon accomplishment, identical protections of rights and institutions would prevail in Northern Ireland whether it remained within the UK or reunified with Ireland; differently put, there was to be a functional equivalence in human, minority, cultural and political rights on both sides of the land border across Ireland.

Through cross-community agreement, the Assembly was entitled to expand its powers; and, with the consent of the UK Secretary of State and the Westminster Parliament, the Assembly may legislate for any function within Westminster's jurisdiction. According to the UK's legal orthodoxies, maximum feasible devolved self-government was therefore within the scope of the local decision-makers. The Northern Ireland Act 1998 permits the Assembly to expand its autonomy regarding *reserved* matters, which included the criminal law, criminal justice, and policing. In 2010 policing and the administration of justice were included among its functions, prompted by the two sovereign governments but at the insistence of Sinn Féin.[10] If the Agreement had been fully implemented, and its potential to expand regional autonomy exploited, then most discretionary public policy in Ireland, north and south, would have been made without direct British ministerial involvement. The London Treasury's budgetary allocation has remained crucial, however, in a region which remains much less economically developed than Great Britain or sovereign Ireland.

Interim Evaluations

The long and turbulent record of implementing and attempted renegotiation of the Agreement has been the subject of several studies (O'Leary, 2019c; Ó Dochartaigh, 2015; Todd, 2013, 2017). In this journal it has been argued that Northern Ireland's novel consociational design, especially its executive, worked better than many had expected, and significantly better than various centripetal arrangements that have been tried or proposed in Northern Ireland and elsewhere (McCulloch, 2013; McGarry & O'Leary, 2015). This judgment remains robust despite all current difficulties.

1998–2016. Despite significant teething difficulties, the DUP's participation in the new institutions was one measure of the Agreement's promise of endurance. The DUP quickly switched from outright opposition to seeking to renegotiate the Agreement, offering itself in the June 1998 Assembly election, as unionists' 'best guarantee' that their interests would be protected in the new regime (DUP, 1998). The party thereby proclaimed its intent to act as 'an ethnic tribune party' (Mitchell, Evans, & O'Leary, 2009). The DUP took the ministerial portfolios to which it was entitled, though it later began to rotate nominees through the cabinet in protest at the failure of the IRA to decommission it arsenal. But it would formally work the Agreement, after the Saint Andrews Agreement of 2006 made some minor amendments, the most significant being the abolition of the concurrent majority requirement to elect the First Minister and Deputy First Minister with the endorsement of both registered nationalists and unionists.[11] Since then, registered nationalists, unionists, and others, have been free to vote for their own leaders, and have had no formal right to veto other parties' choices of leaders. The executive design has throughout incentivized hard-liners to win ministries and the two premierships by partially moderating their platforms and accommodating one another (Mitchell et al., 2009). Negotiations over the placements of ministers in specific portfolios, in principle, were not required because the parties' shares of portfolios, and their choices among them, were determined by the automatic proportional and sequential provisions of the d'Hondt allocation rule.

Most of the Agreement's specifically peace-related provisions were eventually implemented: ceasefires, decommissioning, followed by the substantive disbanding of major paramilitary organizations (notably the IRA); the early release of paramilitaries from jail provided their organizations remained on cease-fire; and highly significant police and judicial reforms (cultural Catholics are now a bare majority of justices on the high court). Police reform would have gone further had the Conservative Secretary of State Owen Patterson not decided in 2011 to end the rigorous quota on recruitment of cultural Catholics at a proportion of 50%. That quota, and other significant reforms, had made significant inroads into transforming the previously partisan police force into a representative service.

The North-South Ministerial Council, as expected, has proven more significant than the British-Irish Council, but cannot be judged to have played a transformative role in relations between the two parts of Ireland—see the appraisals by John Bradley and John Coakley in this volume. The functioning of the NSMC has, however, proved that unionists' fears of its capacities were unfounded. Unionists have used their veto powers to prevent any imaginative extensions of the joint functions and joint implementation bodies. The independent commissions established under the Agreement have had some significant successes (Walsh, 2017), and exemplify the important roles that outsiders can play in constructive engagements in peace processes (McGarry & O'Leary, 2006a, 2006b; Walsh & Doyle,

2018). The least successful has been the Human Rights Commission, which has failed to deliver, under different leaderships, on the admittedly hard task of producing an agreed Bill of Rights tailor-made for local conditions, and capable of being implemented by the Northern Assembly or Westminster.

Equally positively, it was widely noted, except by those hostile to consociation, that although the DUP and Sinn Féin grew in strength, displacing their moderate rivals from their leading positions in their respective blocs, they did so on moderated rather than on more hardline platforms.[12] Sinn Féin increasingly resembled the SDLP; the DUP increasingly resembled the UUP. Though the May 2016 Assembly election had the lowest turnout under the new regime, that datum was compatible with evidence of the calming, and indeed apathetic de-politicization occasionally attributed to consociations (see Table 1). The outcome arguably suggested Northern Ireland's normalization: lower turnouts and greater estrangement from party politics made it more like many of the peaceful, stable, and duller European democracies (Mair, 2013). The vote for all of the major parties was down, but with a significant dip in the first-preference vote for both nationalist parties, partly attributable to leakage to single-issue parties and left-wing organizations: 40 nationalist MLAs were returned, the lowest number since 1998. Turnout was down in all nationalist-majority constituencies. The beneficiaries were the smaller parties. The Greens now had two MLAs instead of one, and the People Before Profits Alliance (PBPA) won two MLAs at the expense of Sinn Féin. The deepening of Northern nationalism appeared to have paused.

Turnout rose in unionist majority constituencies, but not necessarily for the larger unionist parties. The DUP won 38 seats in the 108 seat Assembly, once again, and had sufficient MLAs within its own ranks to use a petition of concern to block any proposals adverse to its interests. The party's new leader, Arlene Foster, in office since January, seemed secure. The UUP, the SDLP, and the Alliance had promised to go into opposition, but this move had not improved their vote share, or increased turnout. These results suggested stagnation among the established parties, and indicated a possible partial demobilization of the Sinn Féin vote consequent upon its moderation in government, especially in Belfast and Derry.

However, throughout 1998–2016 the Agreement stood in constant need of British and Irish maintenance. Successive time-outs, conferences, and accords were needed to resolve impasses, and each looked suspiciously similar to its precursors. Sinn Féin's Deputy First Minister Martin McGuinness considered resigning before the Hillsborough

Table 1. The Northern Ireland Assembly Elections, 2016–2017

First-preference vote share (%)	Unionists			Others			Nationalists	
	TUV	DUP	UUP	APNI	Greens	PBPA	SDLP	SF
2016	3.5	29.2	12.6	7.0	2.7	2.0	12.0	24.0
2017	2.6	28.1	12.9	9.1	2.3	1.8	11.9	27.9
Net gain/loss	−0.9	−1.1	−0.3	+2.1	−0.4	−0.2	−0.1	+3.9

Notes: First-preference vote (%) by bloc and by party. Micro-parties and independents excluded.
Turnout 2016: 54.9%; 2017: 64.8%.
Source: O'Leary (2019c).

Agreement (2010) resolved the delegation of policing and justice powers. The Haass-O'Sullivan talks (2013), and then the Stormont House Agreement of a year later (2014), sought to address flags, parades, and an array of cultural antagonisms, including dealing with the past. The Fresh Start Agreement (2015) tried to re-resolve these matters and a standoff over British and DUP insistence on welfare cuts to which Sinn Féin was opposed, and tackling residual paramilitarism (Mitchell, Tannam, & Wallace, 2018). All the major parties have at different times either refused to abide by the rules, explicitly or implicitly, or have collapsed the executive through refusing to form a government, encouraging a suspension, or by enforcing snap elections through the resignation of one of the first ministers. Since 2010, unionists have refused to participate in the executive if a nationalist minister oversaw justice and policing through the normal working of the d'Hondt allocation process. Later, First Minister Peter Robinson of the DUP, rotated his party's nominees through ministries at a rapid rate, returning to the DUP's initial stratagem in 1999–2002, thereby making a mockery of their roles, and triggering a review of the Agreement. After the Assembly elections of March 2017, Sinn Féin refused to nominate a Deputy First Minister to replace the late Martin McGuinness, or to cooperate in executive formation, unless certain procedural and policy preconditions were met. This decision eventually obliged negotiations that as yet have failed to produce a new executive, though they did come close to success in early 2018, until the DUP leadership withdrew from what it had agreed with Sinn Féin.

2016–2018: Although the Agreement produced many successes from 1998 to 2016, not least peace, institutional instability has been radically exacerbated by UKEXIT. Across Northern Ireland in the referendum called by the Cameron-led Conservative government in the UK those who voted to remain in the EU defeated those who wished to leave by 56–44% in June 2016 (see Table 2). After the referendum in both Scotland and Northern Ireland, there were sustained calls for their respective remain majority-votes to be respected. In the interim Cameron had resigned ignominiously, while Theresa May, his unexpected successor, quickly and emphatically rejected differentiated options. The UK as a whole had voted to leave, she said; ergo, the UK as a whole would leave: 'Brexit means Brexit,' became her mantra, issued at any awkward moment, and there were a lot of them. The United Kingdom of Great Britain, i.e. the Union of England and Scotland, was split, however, as Table 2 demonstrates. England (and Wales) favoured leaving, Scotland did not, i.e. Great Britain was not in agreement with itself. The Union of Great Britain and Northern Ireland displayed a similar pattern; i.e. the larger partner, treated as an

Table 2. The 2016 EU referendum outcomes in the constitutionally distinct territories of the United Kingdom and Gibraltar.

Units in which ballots were counted	Per cent voting to leave the EU	Per cent voting to remain in the EU
United Kingdom & Gibraltar	51.9	48.1
England	53.4	46.6
Wales	52.5	47.5
Northern Ireland	44.2	55.8
Scotland	38.0	62.0
Gibraltar	4.1	95.9

Source: O'Leary (2016, p. 522).

aggregate, wanted to leave, the smaller chose remain. Enforcing the exit of the entire UK therefore means over-riding the preferences of majorities in two of the UK's four units.

In her first visit to Northern Ireland as Prime Minister in July 2016 May declared that 'nobody wants to return to the borders of the past,' but the question now was what the borders of the future would be like. Questions related to future border(s) are handled elsewhere in this volume and in the author's work-in-press (O'Leary, 2019c), but in 1998 all Northern Irish futures had presupposed a European roof. The recital to the treaty protecting the Agreement referred to the British and Irish governments' wish to 'develop still further the unique relationship between their peoples and the close cooperation between their countries as friendly neighbours and as partners in the European Union.' The Downing Street Declaration (1993) had followed both states' accession to the EU in the Maastricht Treaty. The North-South Ministerial Council was explicitly mandated to address 'EU issues.' The Agreement was peppered with references to the European Convention on Human Right and Fundamental Freedoms. All that has now been jeopardized. Differently put, the 1998 Agreement has become part of the collateral damage of the referendum on EU membership in 2016.

As observed by Micheál Martin, the leader of Fianna Fáil, the current leader of the Irish Opposition, 'the text of the agreement and its enabling legislation explicitly requires the Assembly and Executive to operate in accordance with EU law' (McGee, 2018). How can that requirement be met unless Northern Ireland remains within the single market, the customs union and under the jurisdiction of the Court of Justice of the EU? We have here a clash of mandates. Northern Ireland endorsed the Agreement in 1998 and voted to remain in the EU in 2016, whereas Great Britain (driven by England, not Scotland) has voted to leave the EU without considering the impact on the previous Agreement and the treaty protecting it. The Conservatives and the DUP conveniently confine the majority consent principle in the 1998 Agreement to the question of whether Northern Ireland is to remain under UK sovereignty or reunify with Ireland; they appear to think that any other provision of the Agreement may be freely modified by the Westminster parliament. In any case, what leaving the EU meant had hardly been clarified in the conduct of the referendum as both 'soft' and 'hard' options were canvassed by those who wanted to leave.

The DUP had not expected to be on the winning side of the referendum vote. It had had an ideological free ride, not expecting to have to manage the repercussions of a leave vote. The possible consequences—departure from the single market, the customs union, and the termination of numerous EU programs, not least in agriculture, had scarcely been thought about, let alone thought through by DUP politicians (as opposed to some civil servants). The joint executive agreed that there were common dangers to the local economy, but the two governing parties in the North now held diametrically opposed perspectives on the merits of staying in the EU, certain to be the dominant question shaping political life for the next decade. The question equally divided the two sovereign governments.

Sinn Féin called for a referendum on Irish unity in the aftermath of the EU referendum vote, but was not surprised when that the request was refused. McGuinness, however, triggered fresh Assembly elections, confident of the consequences, less than six months later. He resigned early in January 2017, and his party refused to nominate a new Deputy First Minister, thereby obliging snap elections six weeks later. The full *casus belli* for McGuinness's decision, was provided by the Renewable Heating Initiative (RHI), and the attendant scandal, which had threatened to engulf Foster. Applications for what was seen as easy money—'cash for ash'—increased, perhaps especially among those close to DUP

MLAs, or DUP special advisors, though causal connections remain to be fully investigated or proven. Whistleblowers claimed that the scheme was costing millions. The Assembly's Public Accounts Committee found serious inadequacies within the relevant ministries, and Foster was called to appear before the Public Accounts Committee by the SDLP's new leader Colum Eastwood. So far, there had been no proof and little suggestion of personal impropriety on Foster's part, but her refusal to step down gave an impression of a lack of humility that was grating, and not just to nationalists. After all, Robinson had set an appropriate precedent on a previous occasion—stepping aside while an inquiry was conducted into his wife's affairs. This time, however, Sinn Féin did not leave the DUP to sort out its own leadership questions, partly because it felt that Foster's rigidity left it no choice. McGuinness was terminally ill but seized a strategic opportunity, letting rip in his resignation speech,

> The equality, mutual respect and all-Ireland approaches enshrined in the Good Friday Agreement have never been fully embraced by the DUP … [and] the refusal of Arlene Foster to recognize the public anger or to exhibit any humility in the context of the RHI scandal is indicative of a deep-seated arrogance … (McGuinness, 2017)

DUP Communities Minister Paul Givan decision just before the Assembly's dissolution to block a customary £50,000 grant for Líofa, a program enabling children from deprived backgrounds to go to the (Irish-speaking) Gaeltacht on holiday,[13] had added insult to injury. It seemed that respect for the Irish language was beyond the capacity of the DUP. Sinn Féin Finance Minister Máirtín Ó Muilleoir described Givan's decision as the last straw that led McGuinness to trigger elections (Smyth, 2017).

McGuinness did not participate in the campaign, and upon the announcement of his retirement, Ian Paisley Jr was generous, and sincerely gracious beyond public expectation.[14] The remarkable bond forged between the two families would, however, have no future political consequences. McGuinness died on 21 March, 19 days after the Assembly elections. On an increased turnout—see Table 1—Sinn Féin galvanized its base, enhanced its votes and seats, and came within a whisker of pipping the DUP for the position of the largest party, which is entitled to nominate the First Minister. The party obtained its highest ever total vote share in an Assembly election, and came within 1,168 of matching the DUP's first-preference vote. Sinn Féin returned 1 MLA less than the DUP. By contrast, the 2017 Assembly election was a bad experience for all unionists. If the executive had been formed after the elections, either with a four-party grand coalition or a DUP-Sinn Féin diarchy, nationalists and unionists would have had exactly equal numbers of portfolios (see Table 3(a,b)). There was no unionist majority anywhere: in the executive; among registered MLAs; or among voters. By Northern Ireland standards these were major electoral shifts, especially within one year.

The DUP was on the defensive throughout the campaign. Foster attempted to portray Michelle O'Neill, McGuinness's successor as Sinn Féin Assembly leader, as a glove-puppet of Gerry Adams, and freely used Paisley Senior's most famous word: the DUP would *never* agree to a stand-alone Irish Language Act. Foster did take the courteous and prudent step of attending McGuinness's funeral, and reciprocated when O'Neill sought to engage her. Chastened by her electoral experience, Foster looked one step from her political grave: any unexpected revelations in the RHI inquiry would oblige her to resign. But Theresa May, wholly unintentionally, would rescue Foster and the DUP

Table 3. (a) Implicit d'Hondt allocation of eight executive portfolios[a]

d'Hondt divisor	DUP	Sinn Féin	SDLP	UUP	APNI
1	28.0 (1)	27.0 (2)	12.0 (5)	10.0 (6)	8.0
2	14.0 (3)	13.5 (4)	6.0		5.0
3	9.3 (7)	9.0 (8)			
4	7.0	6.27			
Total ministries	3	3	1	1	

[a]Subsequent to the 2017 Assembly elections, if all parties take their entitlements, excluding the Executive Office. Numbers in first row = Number of MLAs per party. Numbers in brackets are the order in which parties would choose ministerial portfolios.

Notes: Through the Departments Act (Northern Ireland) 2016, the number of ministries has been reduced to eight going forward, and the Office of the First Minister and Deputy First Minister was renamed the Executive Office: these simulations assume that eight ministries will be filled by d'Hondt. http://www.legislation.gov.uk/nia/2016/5

Source: O'Leary (2019c).

(b) Implicit d'Hondt allocation of executive portfolios[b]

d'Hondt divisor	DUP	Sinn Féin
1	28.0 (1)	27.0 (2)
2	14.0 (3)	13.5 (4)
3	7.3 (5)	9.0 (6)
4	7.0 (7)	6.75 (8)
Total ministries	4	4

[b]Subsequent to 2017 Assembly elections, if only the DUP and Sinn Féin go into government and take the eight available portfolios. Numbers in first row = Number of MLAs per party. Numbers in brackets are the order in which parties would choose ministerial portfolios.

Source: O'Leary (2019c).

Table 4. The Westminster Elections in Northern Ireland, 2015 and 2017[a]

Vote share (%)	Unionists			Others			Nationalists	
	TUV	DUP	UUP	APNI	Greens	PBPA	SDLP	SF
Vote share 2015	2.3	25.7	16.0	8.6	1.0	0.9	12.0	24.0
Vote share 2017	0.4	36.0	10.3	7.9	0.9	0.7	11.7	29.4
Seats won 2015	0	8	2	0	0	0	3	4
Seats won 2017	0	10	0	0	0	0	0	7
Net gain/loss votes	−1.9	+10.3	−5.7	−0.7	−0.4	−0.2	−0.1	+3.9
Net gain/loss seats		+ 2	−2				−3	+3

[a]Votes by bloc and by party. Micro-parties and independents excluded.

Source: O'Leary (2019c).

from their shell-shocked short-run predicaments. In April 2017, the Conservative Prime Minister triggered a snap Westminster election to take place in early June. Led by the party's Westminster leader, Nigel Dodds, the DUP had a very successful campaign. As

Table 4 shows, the party won 10 of Northern Ireland's seats, its best ever performance. But so did Sinn Féin: there are now no Northern nationalist MPs that take their seats at Westminster for the first time since before the most recent conflict. In contrast, the Conservative party lost disastrously in comparison with pre-election polls and in response it felt obliged to make a confidence and supply arrangement with the DUP.

As this article went to press, Arlene Foster called for the reintroduction of British direct rule over Northern Ireland, after her party's grassroots—or its Westminster MPs—balked at having to accept the passage of an Irish Language Act as part of a possible re-set of relations between the DUP and Sinn Féin. The new leader of Sinn Féin, Mary Lou McDonald, the successor to Gerry Adams, and her Northern deputy Michelle O'Neill, the successor to the late Martin McGuinness, argue—correctly—that reintroducing direct rule would be a breach of both the Agreement and the Saint Andrews Agreement. It would require legislation by Westminster that would enjoy no support from the Dublin government. What currently applies therefore is undeclared direct rule, 'direct rule without direct rule,' i.e. while efforts to reestablish a functioning executive are periodically made civil servants in Belfast and London will make essential decisions.

The deterioration in political cooperation in the North after June 2016 should not be solely assigned to the DUP or Sinn Féin, or to the process of UKEXIT, though the latter has worsened inter-ethnic and international relations. At least some of the blame attaches to the stewardship of the London and Dublin governments, especially since 2010, under Conservative and Fine Gael led administrations. In the early phases of implementing the Agreement both the UK and Irish prime ministers met regularly in the British-Irish Intergovernmental Conference (B-IGC), to coax all parties and republican and loyalist militias successfully into the completion of most of their obligations. The B-IGC *subsumes* both the Anglo-Irish Intergovernmental Council and the Intergovernmental Conference established under the 1985 Agreement, and it may recover its importance in future, after having fallen into desuetude—because of a joint determination by London and Dublin to oblige the local parties to manage Northern Ireland, and to neglect the conference to encourage the DUP to work the Agreement. That was a major strategic error on the part of Dublin, because it allowed the DUP to operate without fear of Dublin's oversight. It was compatible, however, with the Conservatives' ideological preoccupations with sovereignty (and the record of many of its Secretaries of State, including Paterson and Villiers, in opposing Labour's shepherding of the Good Friday Agreement, which the Tories often portrayed as being soft on terrorism.) The possible agenda of the B-IGC is best understood as 'the totality of relationships' between Great Britain and Ireland, '*minus* the exclusively devolved powers of the Assembly.' Under the provisions of the Agreement, the Conference must review the international treaty and the machinery and institutions 'established under it;' and *all-island* and *cross-border* aspects of rights, justice, prisons, and policing are part of its remit. We may therefore expect calls for its revival, especially under a new London government, or if the Northern executive is not reformed, and simply because UK and Irish ministers will no longer be meeting under the auspices of the EU.

The Agreement and Ukexit: The Clash of Two Mandates

The 1998 Agreement's institutions derived their legitimacy from two referendums held on the same day in Ireland that ratified their constitutionality within and without Northern Ireland. The results of these referenda now directly clash with the 2016 referendum on

UKEXIT. The informed Irish nationalist understanding was that Northern Ireland's current status as part of the UK was now a function of Irish choices, not merely the outcome of past British conquest or imposition—including its status within the EU. Northern Ireland was not a province of the UK, being granted devolved authority; rather, it was now, at least potentially, a 'federacy.' That is, federal-like arrangements had been agreed that could not be unilaterally altered by the Westminster parliament. Westminster's sovereignty was qualified; henceforth it had to be exercised in accordance with, and with respect for, the new Agreement and its new institutions, including the roles of Ireland's government in those institutions, all of them respecting Irish self-determination, North and South, conjoint and several.

That was not the reading of unionist lawyers, and the subsequent actions of Unionist parties, both the UUP and the DUP, and the Conservatives, may be profitably read as incremental steps to subvert the plain reading of the Agreement. The sovereignty of the Westminster parliament has always practically meant the paramountcy of England—throughout the history of its Unions and throughout its empire, and the inability of the English to establish entrenched constitutional arrangements with others, both within and outside its Unions, i.e. arrangements that are entrenched beyond the discretion of a simple governing majority in Westminster's House of Commons, has been brutally re-advertised in the course of UKEXIT. Justice Maguire in Belfast in October 2016,[15] and subsequently the UK Supreme Court in January 2017, have effectively declared that Westminster is not tied by the 1998 Agreement, or by the 1998 referendums in both parts of Ireland, to a distinct constitution for Northern Ireland, one that, for instance, would have required legislative consent from the Assembly before the UK began its secession from the EU, even though that secession will necessarily affect the provisions of the Agreement and the powers of the Assembly,[16] and even though the court's predecessors had recognized the Agreement's constitutional character.

The UK courts have effectively declared that Westminster is not constrained in its exit from the EU, neither by how a majority voted in Northern Ireland in the June 2016 referendum, nor by how they voted in 1998—nor or by its solemn treaty with Ireland. A corpus of writings largely emanating from Scots jurists, philosophers and political scientists in which UK Courts were hailed as Europeanized, and recognizing new pluri-national norms, has come to a shuddering halt—writings once embraced by soft unionists and soft nationalists in Scotland and Northern Ireland. The latest court rulings, and the Conservatives' actions, signal that after the UK's departure from the EU, the doctrine of Westminster sovereignty is returning in full force—if it ever went away from the minds of those schooled by AV Dicey (McCrudden & Halberstam, 2017a, 2017b). What may seem arcane legalism matters because the Agreement has been thereby destabilized. The UK's unconstitutionalized system—in which no constitutional, basic or organic law inhibits its Parliament from legislating as it sees fit—will likely be even more destabilizing going forward than it was during the first suspension crises of the early part of this century. The intermittent suspension of the institutions under Labour governments between 2000 and 2006 emphatically broke the Agreement, partly because the deed was performed unilaterally, but it was at least plausibly excused by efforts to create the conditions for the Agreement to work, i.e. by a doctrine of necessity. Today, however, the prospect of UKEXIT, as interpreted by the governing Conservatives, their DUP allies, and the UK courts, has damaged the settled expectations that accompanied the Agreement, namely, joint membership of the EU by the two sovereign governments, joint commitments to the European Convention on Human Rights and Freedoms, and an invisible land border across Ireland. Westminster's decision to modify the terms of the UK's relations with Ireland and the EU will likely weaken all parties' commitments to the institutions negotiated in 1998–2007, despite all protestations to the contrary.

It is an analytical truth that the Agreement *in all its parts* cannot be maintained if the UK leaves the EU, despite solemn assertions to the contrary by both the UK government and the EU-27 in the draft withdrawal agreement (The European Union and the Government of the United Kingdom and Great Britain and Northern Ireland, 2018). The best that can be done to stay close to the ethos of the Agreement is a UKEXITINO, a UKEXIT in name only, in which the UK stays in the single market, the customs union, and accepts the jurisdiction of the Court of Justice of the EU, thereby preventing any need for a fresh re-hardening of the border across Ireland but overturning three of the desiderata upon which May's government has so far insisted.

When one party starts unilaterally to modify a contract, others usually follow. And in this case, the UK Supreme Court's decision in *Miller* that Parliament can quickly do whatever it wants, even though the London executive may not, 'signals to the EU-27 that *any* supposedly binding international agreements the UK enters into can be easily ignored by a future Parliament, without any domestic judicial remedy.'[17] Further institutional instability must now be expected. Given Ireland's success in placing the stabilization of the Agreement in the first basket of issues addressed by Michel Barnier's EU negotiating team in its interaction with the UK's secessionists, and its subsequent success in the provisions regarding the draft Protocol regarding Northern Ireland in the draft withdrawal agreement (The European Union and the Government of the United Kingdom of Great Britain and Northern Ireland, 2018) it would be incoherent for an Irish government directly to collaborate in the reintroduction of British direct rule. But if it occurred, it would be significantly attributable to the UK's decision to leave the EU. The Dublin government wants Northern nationalists to be in the Northern executive, to argue their corner as the UK seeks to leave the EU, and thereby help to minimize the damage to both parts of Ireland. But if Sinn Féin renewed its participation in the Executive, could it do so without insisting that EU-related concessions be made to the North? And are such concessions ones which the DUP can accommodate, quietly or otherwise? Wouldn't the Northern voice on UKEXIT be incurably double-tongued?

If direct rule is re-established, however, that should increase, as noted above, the importance of the B-IGC, in which Dublin would seek to be consulted on all aspect of public policy affecting Northern Ireland, certainly all non-devolved functions, and on devolved functions if the Executive and Assembly are suspended, which may enrage the DUP, which tends to be oblivious to the fact that it is bound by the 1998 Agreement.[18] Given the current Conservative-DUP parliamentary alliance talks to restore the Northern executive, without a formal suspension, may continue as long as may be necessary because that way the London government avoids having to choose between offending the DUP or the Dublin government—and breaking the Agreement. An end to the current impasse could occur either after the UK's formal exit from the EU, or after the termination of the Conservative-DUP supply and confidence arrangement.

The reformation of the power-sharing executive in the North presupposes that both the DUP and Sinn Féin will work with whatever outcome finally emerges from the UK's negotiations with the EU-27. That remains to be tested. Fresh elections in Ireland have to occur by April 2021, but may occur as early as the Autumn of 2018, and may give Sinn Féin greater freedom of maneuver to rejoin the executive with the DUP. Three possibilities are foreseeable, barring an unlikely poll-toping performance by Sinn Féin in the South: the party could have a supply and confidence role supporting a Dublin government led by Fianna Fáil (or Fine Gael), thereby matching the DUP's recent arrangements with London; Sinn Féin could be part of a coalition government in the South; or, returning to another spell in opposition, Sinn Féin may feel less constrained in rejoining the Northern executive.

No prediction will be made about which party blinks first, if any, in negotiations to restore the Belfast executive. The elements of a possible deal are known—a return to a Fresh Start; spending the unexpected booty the DUP has obtained from the UK Treasury through its pact with the Conservatives; an Irish Language Act to be passed at Westminster if not in Belfast, or a general languages act to be passed in Belfast; changing the titles of the First and Deputy First Ministers to Joint First Ministers, to acknowledge reality, and to soften any future loss to the DUP; leaving Foster's status to be decided by the outcome of the public inquiry; and agreement on how to navigate the complex issues attached to UKEXIT. The major party leaders cannot, however, openly discuss key underlying tensions. The bulk of the DUP wants a hard exit, to restore the UK's differences from Ireland; its cadres privately want a hard border, despite the hardships their voters would incur. But the party will publicly accept a soft exit, provided Northern Ireland is not treated differently to Great Britain. Sinn Féin wants the Remain vote respected, but, if UKEXIT occurs, it wants special status for Northern Ireland. Its cadres privately want Northern Ireland to fail to strengthen the case for reunification, and may prefer to polarize choices between direct rule under the Conservatives and a reunited Ireland within the EU. It follows that there will likely be further electoral polarization in the North; competition will intensify between the DUP and Sinn Féin, weakening further the SDLP and the UUP.

Consociationalism and The Agreement in 2018

Though now is not a good moment for Northern Ireland's consociation, the experience is not yet over, so a definitive reckoning must be postponed. Many criticisms of consociation, however, are based on false observations or assumptions. For example, question-time procedures to interrogate ministers, even when there was a grand coalition in the North between 2007 and 2016, showed that consociation need not preclude effective parliamentary oversight (Conley, 2013). Parties are not, contrary to rumour, obliged to take their portfolios; what they cannot do is exclude other parties from taking their entitlements. Contrary to the stalest of clichés, consociation does not eliminate democratic opposition (O'Leary, 2005). Similarly, the destabilizing challenges of UKEXIT do not mean that consociation cannot survive—partly because it is not yet clear with what it would be replaced.

Northern Ireland's peace process and consociational experiment have in fact enabled novel opposition parties to organize in conditions of generalized security. New parties have come and, in some cases, gone. Notable new arrivals have included the Northern Ireland Women's Coalition, the Greens, the People Before Profit Alliance, and NI21. Over time the Alliance has become a more vibrant socially liberal party. Turbulence among 'the others' has not simply been a sign of their futility; their emergence has prompted some of the other parties to update their platforms. Moreover, in 2016 the moderate UUP and the moderate nationalists of the SDLP went into opposition after an all-party review of the Agreement provided resources for that project. It is therefore fallacious to maintain that consociation, especially in Northern Ireland, mandates encompassing grand coalitions, or is incapable of internally agreed changes.

Most fundamentally, consociationalists, realists with a high tolerance for cultural difference, believe that certain collective identities, especially those based on nationality, ethnicity, language, and religion, are generally fairly durable once formed (Goemans, 2013). In Ulster, the nationalist and unionist political identities have been expressed in overt party-political form since the 1880s, and were deeply rooted in earlier settler-native identities developed after the seventeenth century British colonial conquests (O'Leary, 2019a). The promotion of consociation from the 1970s has therefore been an institutional response to the durability of antagonistic identities; it cannot credibly be regarded as their cause, as some currently suggest. Politicians, parties, and communities have interpreted their histories and futures through powerful narratives, myths, and symbols, but these have resonated, and made sense of each community's respective past—they are not mere fictions, to be dispelled by therapy from a liberal educator. Hyper-constructivists are too optimistic about the capacities of political regimes (and persons) to dissolve, transform, or transcend inherited collective identities, certainly with rapidity, and they overemphasize the powers of political manipulators. Additionally, though a cause for regret, voters typically make their party 'choices' based on who they are, rather than what they think (Achen & Bartels, 2016, pp. 232–266).

Necessity is pled in defense of consociations, not cultural pluralism for its own sake. Adversarial democracy on the Westminster model between 1920 and 1972 did not produce alternating governments in Northern Ireland, especially because the opposition had no hope of becoming the government, given the biased partition line drawn to secure a 2:1 Protestant majority. Today it would be a recipe for a different kind of instability. The durability of the local collective antagonistic identities obliges a narrowing of the local institutional options: consociational (or some other power-sharing) democracy *or* no worthwhile democracy (or rule by an outside arbitrator).

Had consociation been negotiated before the local graveyards were filled through armed conflict who can reasonably doubt that matters would be better today? And who can reasonably doubt that there has been greater justice, both egalitarian and proportional, in the last two decades than at any juncture since Northern Ireland was formed? Consociationalists maintain that self-rule and shared rule are possible, and that each consociational partner, in principle, should be free to reform and transform themselves according to their own procedures and chosen pace. Michael Walzer, thinking of the former Ottoman and Hapsburg empires, once suggested that consociation is heroic,

> because it aims to maintain imperial coexistence without the imperial bureaucrats and without the distance that made those bureaucrats more or less impartial rulers ... the different groups have to tolerate one another and work out among themselves the terms of their coexistence. (1997, p. 22)

An heroic enterprise has been underway since 1998, arguably with too few heroes to sustain it.

In his account of the breakdown of consociation in the Netherlands Arend Lijphart emphasized that the social cleavages between the blocs lost their intensity (Lijphart, 1975) Declines took place in support for bloc parties, accompanying social 'de-pillarization.' Neutral media began to prevail over each historic bloc's partisan internal communications. Secularization proceeded apace, especially among Catholics, facilitating both joint Christian party alliances, and the weakening of the religious-secular cleavage. The rejection, especially on the left, of consociational rules of the game, and the promotion of adversarial and more majoritarian politics mattered, as did increased support for less deferential politics. Broadly speaking, political elites, challenged from below, weakened by region-wide list-PR that encouraged party fragmentation, abandoned the politics of accommodation, both as the depth of the original animating cleavages faded, and as cross-cutting and overlap among preferences and communities increased. As Lijphart emphasized, 'not the least of the virtues of politics of accommodation is that it provides the means for its own [peaceful] abolition' (Lijphart, 1975, p. 219).

Analogous conditions do not exist in Northern Ireland, at least not yet. The cleavage between the two major blocs remains intense, though calmer than 20 years ago. It is an ethno-national cleavage, in which the blocs identify with rival nations, with roots in a colonial encounter between natives and settlers, and in which religious differences reinforce the national cleavage. Inter-bloc trust is some distance away. Secularization is taking place, especially fast-paced among Catholics, but without the same consequences as in the Netherlands because ex-Catholics largely identify as Irish, whereas ex-Protestants largely identify as British. De-pillarization is limited—there remains extensive residential, and schooling segregation, although there are now much more mixed workplaces, both in the public and the private sectors, and there has been increased inter-group marriage. Residential segregation and denominational schooling are both partly voluntary and market-driven, and difficult to change through public policy without a stronger cross-community consensus. Integrated schooling is available, but not extensively chosen. Integration as an objective is piously upheld, but the question remains: integration into what? Into the UK, Northern Ireland, or Ireland? Into a British, Northern Irish, or Irish identity, or some permutation thereof? The new political arrangements have led to greater calm, and to greater public expression of identities that are neither nationalist nor unionist, but these are not, at least not yet, strongly mobilized into party politics. There is some evidence of a Northern Irish identity, a potentially complementary identity for all, one that may have increased in expression because of the 1998 Agreement (Garry, 2009), but its meanings are debatable, and the party that tried to build on this prospectus, NI21 (Twenty-First Century Northern Ireland), could not decide whether to be unionist or other, and collapsed amid in-fighting and a scandal.

The ethno-national cleavage is likely to be enhanced by UKEXIT, not reduced. The remain-leave cleavage on the EU will manifest itself with decreasing contentment with the UK, especially among educated Catholics. The existing institutions and the electoral system make party elites responsive to their voters' concerns, which remain more traditionally nationally minded than cosmopolitan liberals, socialists, and ecologists would like. The welcome addition of feminism to the mix merely adds republican feminists, social democratic nationalist feminists, liberal Alliance feminists, and unionist and loyalist feminists to the story (the Northern Ireland Women's Coalition did not long survive the service it performed in making the 1998 Agreement) (Cowell-Myers, 2011; Murtagh, 2008). The left–or left(s)–remain(s) as divided on the national question as the right(s).

The centre, however, has moved. The Alliance was once clearly pro-Union, but now stands less certainly for letting Northern Ireland's status be decided by a majority. That enables its usually highly educated liberals to coexist peacefully, and prevents its collapse into a small party of Protestant liberals. Social liberalism may help cross-cut identities—

Sinn Féin and Alliance are more vigorous in supporting women's rights, LGBT rights, and same-sex marriage, than are other parties. The DUP almost monopolizes the traditionalist stance on these questions among Protestants. The SDLP has moved more slowly and less visibly on these subjects than Sinn Féin, reflecting its older electorate.

Two key features of consociations are the principles of parity and proportionality, but they are rarely identical in their implications. Groups vary in size, so their proportional weights and demands differ. Parity implies equality, in status, in esteem, in power. It is tough for formerly dominant groups to grant to a group that was once inferior. In Northern Ireland parity between the two core groups is yet to be fully attained—most unionists have refused to interpret the 1998 Agreement as a bi-national settlement, with concomitant consequences for parading, the display of flags, emblems, and insignia, and the status of Irish. Yet the proportions of the two peoples have been slowly changing since 1961. It is entirely possible to see those who vote for Northern nationalist parties not only becoming the greater number, but also on average being better educated, and therefore better prepared for competitive life in contemporary capitalism. The period ahead will test whether unionists can accommodate both proportionality and parity, and falls in relative socio-economic status. Can they leave the last lingering shades of supremacy and embrace equality? If they can, they may keep Northern Ireland in the Union; if they can't, they will almost certainly undermine their own standing and herald not just the twilight, but the demise of the UK. Sinn Féin's most famous slogan in Irish is *Tiocfaidh ár lá*. It means, 'Our day will come,' i.e. Irish reunification will come. The current species of English nationalism, especially outside of London, that is driving UKEXIT, and currently making no significant concessions to Scotland and Northern Ireland, may achieve Sinn Féin's major goal more effectively than IRA violence ever did.

The consociation negotiated in 1998 materialized because key leaders of the formerly dominant majority decided to appease the demographically expanding minority, then on the verge of altering the balance of power in the electoral arena. It was an act of strategic prudence. Lijphart regards a dual balance of power as unlikely to promote consociation because each segment's leaders may hope to win a decisive majority, and have insufficient incentives to create a stable consociation (1977, p. 55). This intuition seems sound, and may describe Northern Ireland as this article goes to press, but it requires qualification. If demographic transformations convert the relations between groups from a situation of dominance towards one of dualism, then, other things being equal, the segment that is losing dominance has incentives to consider consociation. Amid the ironies, one merits emphasis. The DUP opposed the consociational design of the Good Friday Agreement, but in the decade ahead it will become the most ardent defender of its veto provisions. On the other side, the ascendant segment may have a clear present interest in preferring a share in power to the uncertainty of winning majority status in the future. But with its historical antagonist seemingly bent on collective self-harm, and intent on treating them, at best, as collateral damage, the historically subaltern Northern Irish Catholics may judge that the breakup of one Union, the UK's with the EU, may lead to the break-up of the two within the UK. That would require cultural Catholics to become more nationalist, turn out more, and vote SDLP, Sinn Féin, or for another other all-island party. The Others would have to follow that trend, to keep their appeal among cultural Catholics, i.e. shift toward being soft nationalists. One can imagine that occurring with both the Alliance and Green party; both parties have moved to become neutral on the Union. Lastly, cultural Catholics are practically a demographic majority in four counties, the two largest cities, and in primary schools. As these facts express themselves electorally in the late 2020s, Northern nationalists may see themselves as an emergent majority. UKEXIT will not make unionists into nationalists, but it seems likely that cultural Catholics will become keener on Irish reunification—to return to the EU, and, more significantly, because they will believe that reunification will improve their life-chances. To be determined.

Two matters have been clarified, however, since Theresa May triggered Article 50 of the Treaty on EU. Northern Ireland will have unique status in its provisions for citizenship. The authorized will continue to be either Irish or British citizens, or both, and through Irish citizenship will retain EU citizenship. The second is that on Irish reunification Northern Ireland would automatically become part of the EU. These clarifications matter. Those keen on returning to the EU, or who are adversely affected by UKEXIT, have incentives to vote for Irish reunification. The old unionist case against Irish reunification had three major components: an independent Ireland meant Rome rule; the Republic was mono-cultural, and unattractive, compared to the multi-national UK; and, the Republic was poorer, pursuing an isolationist and irrational economic policy. Whatever their contestable past truth-content these arguments no longer pass muster. Ireland is de-Catholicizing, and it is multi-cultural and prosperous—multi-cultural because it is prosperous, and vice versa. It is richer than Northern Ireland, absolutely, and per capita, before and after the subvention by the UK treasury is added to the North's ledger. And sovereign Ireland is staying in the world's largest market, which all gravity-weighted models of international trade suggest is the wiser bet. Updated unionist arguments suggest that unifying with Northern Ireland would be so expensive that the South—and its mean-minded pocket-conscious voters— would refuse the responsibility; that exiting the EU will be better for all the British, especially the less well-off; and that membership of the Euro guarantees that Ireland will be in a slow-growth zone, compared to the larger neighbouring island (chock full of inveterate and enthusiastic global traders).

The older arguments were clearly stronger.

Notes

1. The Agreement was called the Belfast Agreement by the UK government and by Ulster Unionists; though made in many places, in the language of treaties it was 'done at Belfast.' Its most popular name worldwide is the Good Friday Agreement (GFA), because it was finalized in plenary on the day commemorating Christ's crucifixion, a mobile date in the Christian calendar.
2. The official name of the Irish state in the English language is Ireland (Constitution of Ireland, 1937 Article 4), not the Republic of Ireland. The official name of the United Kingdom is the United Kingdom of Great Britain and Northern Ireland. One consequence of the Agreement is that both states now recognize each other's official names.
3. In Irish law the enactment of 'the British Irish Agreement' is dated 22 March 1999; in UK law the text of 'the Agreement between the Government of the UK of Great Britain and Northern Ireland and the Government of Ireland' is dated May 2000. The legislative enactments of the treaties are at http://www. irishstatutebook.ie/eli/1999/act/1/enacted/en/html; and http://treaties.fco.gov.uk/docs/pdf/2000/TS0050. The UK text 'Agreement between the Government of the United Kingdom of Great Britain and Northern Ireland and the Government of Ireland' declares it was previously published as Ireland No. 1 (1999) Cm. 4291.
4. Government of the United Kingdom (1998). The former US Senate Majority Leader's memoir is a model of its kind, G. J. Mitchell (2000).
5. *The Northern Ireland Act 1998.* 1998 Chapter 47 http://www.hmso.gov.uk/acts/acts1998/19980047.htm.
6. For introductions to the DUP see Tonge, Braniff, Hennessey, McAuley, and Whiting (2014), and for an earlier account by a former insider see Smyth (1983). For introductions to Sinn Féin see Feeney (2002) and de Bréadún (2015), and for the earlier history of the party see Sweeney (1971) and Laffan (1999).

7. See the details of its current agreement with the Conservatives at the UK government's official web-site: https://www.gov.uk/government/publications/conservative-and-dup-agreement-and-uk-government-financial-support-for-northern-ireland.
8. For why UKEXIT rather than the ubiquitous BREXIT is the appropriate abbreviation see O'Leary (2016).
9. The Agreement therefore met the four criteria of a full consociation (O'Leary, 2005). The partners to this consociation were legally designated in the new Assembly as (British) unionists, (Irish) nationalists, and 'others.'
10. *Excepted* matters, e.g. the Crown and the currency, are beyond the Assembly's remit.
11. Government of Ireland and Government of the United Kingdom of Great Britain and Northern Ireland (2006).
12. The same critics usually argue that consociation obliges entrenchment and freezes all prospects of progressive change; they have some difficulty explaining away the fact that three of Northern Ireland's largest parties, the DUP, Sinn Féin and the Alliance party, are now led by women.
13. Irish language schools are held in summer in the Gaeltacht, similar to US camp programs.
14. https://www.youtube.com/watch?v=DZCWAwnSAtY.
15. 18 October 2016 NIQB 85, Maguire J, available at courtsni.gov.uk.
16. See O'Leary (2019c) for textual evidence of the salience of European matters in the Agreement, its statutory implementation, and the treaty protecting it.
17. McCrudden and Halberstam (2017) at https://wp.me/p1cVqo-1tK.
18. The 1998 Agreement defines the role of the BIIGC as addressing the 'totality of relationships,' and specifically states that it subsumes (the dictionary meaning = 'includes') the IGC of the AIA of 1985 (Government of the United Kingdom, 1998, Strand Three, pp. 1–9), focuses on non-devolved matters, and is embedded in an international treaty, see Agreement between the Government of the United Kingdom of Great Britain and Northern Ireland and the Government of Ireland, Article 2 (iv), (Government of the United Kingdom, 1998, p. 28).

References

Achen, C., & Bartels, L. M. (2016). *Democracy for realists*. Princeton, NJ: Princeton University Press.
Conley, R. S. (2013). The consociational model and question time in the Northern Ireland Assembly: Policy issues, procedural reforms and executive accountability 2007–2011. *Irish Political Studies*, *28*(1), 78–98.
Cowell-Myers, K. (2011). A collarette on a donkey: The Northern Ireland women's coalition and the limitations of contagion theory. *Political Studies*, *59*, 411–431.
de Bréadún, D. (2015). *Power play: The rise of modern Sinn Féin*. Sallins: Merrion Press.
Doyle, J. (Ed.) (2010). *Policing the narrow ground: Lessons from the transformation of policing in Northern Ireland*. Dublin: Royal Irish Academy.
DUP. (1998). Your best guarantee for the future of Northern Ireland. *Assembly Election Manifesto 1998*. Retrieved http://cain.ulst.ac.uk/issues/politics/docs/dup/dup250698.pdf
Elkins, Z., Ginsburg, T., & Melton, J. (2009). *The endurance of national constitutions*. Cambridge: Cambridge University Press.
The European Union, & The Government of the United Kingdom of Great Britain and Northern Ireland. (2018). *Draft agreement on the withdrawal of the United Kingdom of Great Britain and Northern Ireland from the European Union and the European atomic energy community highlighting the progress made (coloured version) in the negotiation round with the UK of 16–19 March 2018*. Brussels.
Feeney, B. (2002). *Sinn Féin: A hundred turbulent years*. Dublin: The O'Brien Press.
Fontana, G. (2017). *Education policy and power-sharing in post-conflict societies: Lebanon, Northern Ireland, and Macedonia*. London: Palgrave Macmillan.
Garry, J. (2009). Consociationalism and its critics: Evidence from the historic Northern Ireland assembly election 2007. *Electoral Studies*, *28*, 458–466.
Goemans, P. (2013). National cultural autonomy: Otto Bauer's challenge to liberal nationalism. In E. Nimni, A. Osipov, & D. J. Smith (Eds.), *The challenge of Non-territorial autonomy: Theory and practice* (pp. 25–38). Oxford: Peter Lang.
Government of Ireland and Government of the United Kingdom of Great Britain and Northern Ireland. (2006, October 11–13). Agreement at St Andrews. Retrieved from https://www.dfa.ie/media/dfa/alldfawebsitemedia/ourrolesandpolicies/northernireland/st-andrews-agreement.pdf

Government of the United Kingdom. (1998). *The Agreement: Agreement reached in the multi-party negotiations.*

Laffan, M. (1999). *The resurrection of Ireland. The Sinn Féin Party, 1916–1923.* Cambridge: Cambridge University Press.

Lijphart, A. (1975). *The politics of accommodation: Pluralism and democracy in the Netherlands* (2nd ed.). Berkeley: University of California Press.

Lijphart, A. (1977). *Democracy in plural societies: A comparative exploration.* New Haven: Yale University Press.

Mair, P. (2013). *Ruling the void? The hollowing of western democracy.* London: Verso.

McCrudden, C., & Halberstam, D. (2017a). *Miller* and Northern Ireland: A critical constitutional response. *Michigan Law: Public Law and Legal Theory Research Paper Series, Paper 575*(October), pp. [also to be published in the UK Supreme Court Yearbook, Volume 8].

McCrudden, C., & Halberstam, D. (2017b, November 21). *Northern Ireland's Supreme Court Brexit problem (and the UK's too).* Retrieved from https://wp.me/p1cVqo-1tK

McCrudden, C., McGarry, J., O'Leary, B., & Schwartz, A. (2016). Why Northern Ireland's institutions need stability. *Government and Opposition, 51*(1), 30–58.

McCulloch, A. (2013). The track record of centripetalism in deeply divided places. In J. McEvoy & B. O'Leary (Eds.), *Power-Sharing in deeply divided places* (pp. 94–111). Philadelphia: University of Pennsylvania Press.

McEvoy, J. (2015). *Power-Sharing executives: Governing in Bosnia, Macedonia and Northern Ireland.* Philadelphia: University of Pennsylvania Press.

McGarry, J., & O'Leary, B. (2004). Policing reform in Northern Ireland. In *The Northern Ireland conflict: Consociational engagements.* Oxford: Oxford University Press.

McGarry, J., & O'Leary, B. (2006a). Consociational theory, Northern Irelands conflict, and its agreement. Part One. What consociationalists can learn from Northern Ireland. *Government and Opposition, 41*(1), 43–63.

McGarry, J., & O'Leary, B. (2006b). Consociational theory, Northern Irelands conflict, and its agreement. Part Two. What anti-consociationalists can learn from Northern Ireland. *Government and Opposition, 41*(2), 249–277.

McGarry, J., & O'Leary, B. (2015). Power-sharing executives: Consociational and centripetal formulae and the case of Northern Ireland. *Ethnopolitics, 15*(5), 497–519. Retrieved from http://dx.doi.org/10.1080/17449057.2015.1088231

McGee, H. (2018, January 13). North must become a 'Special Economic Zone' under Brexit, says Micheál Martin. *Irish Times.*

McGuinness, M. (2017, January 9). Full text of Martin McGuinness's resignation letter. *Irish Times.*

Mitchell, D., Tannam, E., & Wallace, S. (2018, September). The Good Friday agreement and political cooperation. *Irish Political Studies.*

Mitchell, G. J. (2000). *Making peace* (2nd ed.). Berkeley: University of California Press.

Mitchell, P., Evans, G., & O'Leary, B. (2009). Extremist outbidding in ethnic party systems is not inevitable: Tribune parties in Northern Ireland. *Political Studies, 57*(2), 397–421.

Murtagh, C. (2008). A transient transition: The cultural and institutional obstacles impeding the Northern Ireland Women's Coalition in its progression from informal to formal politics. *Irish Political Studies, 23*(1), 21–40.

Ó Dochartaigh, N. (2015). The longest negotiation: British policy, IRA strategy and the making of the Northern Ireland peace settlement. *Political Studies, 63,* 202–220.

O'Leary, B. (1999). The nature of the agreement. *Fordham Journal of International Law, 22*(4 (April)), 1628–1667.

O'Leary, B. (2005). Debating consociational politics: Normative and explanatory arguments. In S. J. R. Noel (Ed.), *From power-sharing to democracy: Post-conflict institutions in ethnically divided societies* (pp. 3–43). Toronto, ON: McGill-Queens University Press.

O'Leary, B. (2016). The Dalriada document: Towards a multinational compromise that respects democratic diversity in the United Kingdom. *The Political Quarterly, 87*(4), 518–533.

O'Leary, B. (2019a). *A treatise on Northern Ireland. Volume 1: Colonialism.* Oxford: Oxford University Press.

O'Leary, B. (2019b). *A treatise on Northern Ireland. Volume 2. Control.* Oxford: Oxford University Press.

O'Leary, B. (2019c). *A treatise on Northern Ireland. Volume 3. Consociation and confederation.* Oxford: Oxford University Press.

O'Leary, B., Grofman, B., & Elklit, J. (2005). Divisor methods for sequential portfolio allocation in multi-party executive bodies: Evidence from Northern Ireland and Denmark. *American Journal of Political Science, 49*(1 (January)), 198–211.

Smyth, C. (1983). *The Ulster Democratic Unionist Party: A case study in political and religious convergence* (PhD). Queen's University of Belfast, Belfast.

Smyth, C. (2017, April 26). Stormont file shows DUP minister was warned over Líofa cut. *The Detail (thedetail), online.*

Sweeney, J. (1971). Why "Sinn Féin?" *Eire-Ireland*, *6*(2), 33–40.

Todd, J. (2013). Thresholds of state change: Changing British state institutions and practices in Northern Ireland after direct rule. *Political Studies*, *62*, 522–538.

Todd, J. (2017). From identity politics to identity change: Exogenous shocks, constitutional moments and the impact of Brexit on the Island of Ireland. *Irish Studies in International Affairs*, *28*, 57–72.

Tonge, J., Braniff, M., Hennessey, T., McAuley, J. W., & Whiting, S. (2014). *The Democratic Unionist Party: From protest to power.* Oxford: Oxford University Press.

Walsh, D. (2017). *Independent commissions and contentious issues in post-good Friday agreement Northern Ireland.* Basingstoke: Palgrave Macmillan.

Walsh, D., & Doyle, J. (2018). External actors in consociational settlements: A re-examination of Lijphart's negative assumptions. *Ethnopolitics*, *17*(1), 21–36.

Walzer, M. (1997). *On toleration.* New Haven, CT: Yale University Press.

Intergovernmental and Cross-Border Civil Service Cooperation: The Good Friday Agreement and Brexit

ETAIN TANNAM

ABSTRACT   This article aims to examine the impact of the Good Friday Agreement on British–Irish intergovernmental cooperation and cross-border Irish/Northern Irish civil cooperation from 2001 to 2017. It also makes provisional observations about Brexit's impact. British–Irish and cross-border cooperation were emphasised as integral to resolving the conflict in Northern Ireland by successive Irish governments and by the Social Democratic and Labour Party in Northern Ireland. Therefore, in assessing the Good Friday Agreement's overall significance, it is essential to examine its impact on administrative and intergovernmental cooperation. It will be shown that Good Friday agreement's institutions for intergovernmental and East–West relations were under-utilised before Brexit and so were not equipped to deal with Brexit's challenges in 2016–2018. However, a legally enshrined institutionalised relationship, whether by empowering the Good Friday's institutions and/ or by creating a new legal agreement, will be needed in the years ahead if and when Brexit happens.

This article examines the impact of the Good Friday Agreement on British–Irish intergovernmental cooperation and cross-border Irish/Northern Irish civil cooperation from 2001 to 2017. It also makes provisional observations about Brexit's impact. British–Irish and cross-border cooperation were emphasised as integral to resolving the conflict in Northern Ireland by successive Irish governments and by the Social Democratic and Labour Party (SDLP) in Northern Ireland. The Three Strands approach devised by John Hume, former leader of the SDLP emphasised reconciling nationalists and unionists and Irish and British citizens as being the key to conflict resolution in Northern Ireland. Taking the EU model of post-war Franco-German cooperation as an example, John Hume emphasised the need to tolerate different identities on the same island and to adopt a non-zero sum approach to nationality, where territorial boundaries were less salient. Conflict resolution then was about achieving cooperation across three sets of relationships: the relationship within Northern Ireland between unionists and nationalists (Strand One); the relationship between Northern Ireland and Ireland (Strand Two) and the relationship between the Irish government and the British government (Strand Three).

The bilateral intergovernmental relationship mattered because the Irish and British governments were kinship states. These governments had resources and formal legitimacy (the UK) to influence Northern Ireland, or informal legitimacy (Ireland). Unionists looked to the British government for protection and nationalists looked to the Irish government for protection. Over decades, neither government had provided this sense of security and guaranteed rights. For Hume, this insecurity had contributed to the development of a discriminatory unionist regime in Northern Ireland from 1922 and of Irish Republican Army (IRA) violence from the 1960s.

The Franco-German model that inspired Hume also gave rise to a specific focus on the role of economic functional interests in driving cooperation, despite historic conflict. The empirical model was explained theoretically by functionalists and by neo-functionalists. The earlier functionalists argued that local communities and grass root communities, seeking to solve common economic problems would bring an end to territorial borders, in the absence of elite incentives (Mitrany, 1975).Theoretically, cooperation can emerge from the existence of new common economic interests that are superimposed on older conflicts of interests and transform the relationship.

For neo-functionalists grass root cooperation will not suffice. Instead, the cooperative process is elite-led by the European Commission in the EU, but it is also a response to grass root, trade and employers' unions demands for increased economic growth and better quality of life (Haas, 1958). Bureaucratic cross-border cooperation was a key feature of the integration process, whereby bureaucracies would become increasingly intermeshed in an interdependent world, where joint implementation of common policies would occur. Thus, both in integration theory's prescriptions for conflict resolution generally and in John Hume's model of conflict resolution in Northern Ireland, cross-border cooperation and British–Irish intergovernmental cooperation are central. Therefore, as O'Leary shows in this volume (O'Leary, 2018), the complex consociationalist Good Friday Agreement provided for institutional cross-border and intergovernmental cooperation. Administrative cooperation between civil service departments matters practically because it is unlikely that significant cross-border cooperation can occur without bureaucratic coordination and management. This article examines administrative aspects of cross-border cooperation, as well as elite level political cooperation.

It is argued that the Good Friday Agreement has had a significant impact on cross-border administrative cooperation, but in itself, it did not cause increased intergovernmental cooperation, as it reflected a strong relationship in the first place. Indeed, this article shows that the process of increasing administrative cooperation was not organic, but was caused by elite level political intergovernmental cooperation. It is argued that to ensure that administrative and intergovernmental cooperation continue in the aftermath of Brexit, greater use of British–Irish institutions is required.

Cooperation is defined as communication, consultation and joint problem solving Intergovernmental cooperation is defined as cooperation between British and Irish heads of government and their ministers. Civil service cooperation is defined as widespread cooperation between civil service departments in Northern Ireland and Ireland to deal with common problems and interests and to explore cooperation in new policy areas, where common interests were not previously perceived to exist. The findings are based on confidential semi-structured interviews with the author in the Irish Department of Foreign Affairs, the Department of the Taoiseach, the Irish Department of Agriculture, the Northern Irish Department of the First Minister and Deputy First Minister, including finance officials, the Special EU Programmes Body (SEUPB), assistants in the Northern Ireland Executive and the Northern

Ireland Office between January and June 2016. Interviews were also conducted with officials in the Cabinet Office in February 2017. In the first section, the weaknesses in cooperation historically are identified and the Good Friday Agreement's relevance to strengthening cooperation is highlighted. In the second section the impact of the Good Friday Agreement is assessed and in the final section, the impact of Brexit is examined.

Intergovernmental and Civil Service Cooperation 1922–1998

Civil service cross-border cooperation did not evolve until the 1990s. From the foundation of the Irish state in 1922 successive Irish governments adopted a policy of boycotting the Northern Ireland administration because of claims that by cooperating with the Northern Ireland civil service and government, the Irish state was legitimising partition. Northern Irish administrators also insulated themselves from the Irish state, as they sought to build a unionist regime (McColgan, 1981).

British–Irish intergovernmental relations were also sensitive. Contact was limited and rhetoric on both sides was reserved and periodically antagonistic. Successive British and Irish governments ignored the failure of democracy in Northern Ireland for many years. When the conflict broke out, Jack Lynch, then Irish prime minister, called for UN intervention. The British government's response was that any Irish, or UN involvement in Northern Ireland was an erosion of UK sovereignty and tensions between governments were extremely high (Ferriter, 2005, p. 628). However, the 1973 Sunningdale Agreement reflected increased British–Irish intergovernmental cooperation and then UK prime minister, Heath 'threw his weight behind the SDLP and Dublin government' (O'Leary, Elliott, & Wilford, 1988, p. 36), but unionist opposition to the Council and especially to the inclusion of policing brought down the Sunningdale Agreement and the late 1970s saw heightened securitisation in Northern Ireland and deteriorating political stability, hindering cross-border and intergovernmental cooperation.

However, in 1985 the Anglo-Irish Agreement institutionalised intergovernmental cooperation (O'Leary & McGarry, 1993), introduced an institutionalised Irish dimension for the first time and altered fundamentally intergovernmental relations, laying the basis for the peace process of the 1990s. The Agreement was a key landmark in the history of the conflict and the British–Irish relationship (Arthur, 2000). Thus, until the early 1980s, there were weak levels of civil service and generally, there were weak levels of intergovernmental cooperation. However, the Anglo-Irish Agreement reflected a new relationship between senior UK and Irish civil servants and leaders and many of the ideas stemmed from joint discussions between key civil servants. British–Irish cooperation and cooperation between the Anglo-Irish Division in the Irish Department of Foreign Affairs, the Cabinet Office and the Northern Ireland Office typified the relationship from this period onwards, culminating in the Good Friday Agreement. However, this cooperation did not extend to other civil service departments, many of which showed a reluctance to cooperate (Tannam, 1999).

In the 1990s, despite rhetoric that EU funding created incentives for cross-border cooperation and that the new Single European Market created further opportunities for cross-border economic cooperation, civil service cross-border cooperation was not widespread. It was limited to specific units in the Northern Ireland Office, the Irish Department of Foreign Affairs, the Department of the Taoiseach and EU units in certain departments.

As regards EU incentives for civil service cooperation in the 1990s, the EU funded various cross-border programmes and made the funding conditional on cross-border cooperation occurring. The EU's logic echoed the functionalist logic of international cooperation, that by providing economic incentives, common interest between states would be upgraded and incentives to politically cooperate would increase. Under EU rules, partners also had to establish monitoring committees to represent local government, relevant civil service departments and the Commission. However, in practice, administrative systems were highly centralised in both jurisdictions and the departments of Finance, the Northern Ireland Office and the Irish Department of Foreign Affairs played the lead roles in governing cross-border cooperation. Similarly, in the EU Programme for Peace and Reconciliation (the 'peace packages'), the British and Irish governments nominated agencies to manage the funding, but approval of the grant allocation was made by the two Finance departments (Tannam, 1999, p. 159). Overall, cross-border civil service cooperation in the 1990s was strongly controlled by the Northern Ireland Office and the Department of Foreign Affairs, the two Finance departments and the Taoiseach department, with the Department of Foreign Affairs being briefed by all Irish departments, including the Taoiseach departments before any initiative was decided (Tannam, 1999, p. 165).

Indeed other departments had scarcely any inclination to cooperate for the following reasons (Tannam, 1999, pp. 160–164): each civil service department and division had its own policy priorities and these were not cross-border; there was limited communication between division within each department and no apparent horizontal coordination in each civil service and there were economic and political conflicts of interest between departments in Northern Ireland and in Ireland, for example in tourism. Thus, the Northern Ireland Office and the Irish Department of Foreign Affairs took the lead in trying to encourage cooperation, but there was little widespread departmental cross border cooperation. In contrast, the Good Friday Agreement provided for institutional cross-border cooperation that was intended to involve many civil service departments, not simply the Northern Ireland Office, the Irish Department of Foreign Affairs.

The Good Friday Agreement's Provisions for Intergovernmental and Civil Service Cooperation

The Good Friday Agreement provided for significant institutional innovation in the Irish and Northern Irish civil service and in UK–Irish intergovernmental relations. As regards British–Irish intergovernmental cooperation, the British–Irish Council provided a forum for both heads of government to discuss common economic interests with Welsh, Northern Irish, Scottish and Crown Dependencies executive heads. These institutions reflected the Hume approach of widening and deepening between the islands so that a perception of shared identities and interests could exist, but of also institutionalising the role of the kinship state governments—UK and Irish governments. The British–Irish Intergovernmental Conference subsumed the Anglo-Irish Agreement's Intergovernmental Conference and the earlier Anglo-Irish Conference and represents UK and Irish governments, comprising heads of government, ministers and senior civil servants. The Irish government has a special role in the British–Irish Intergovernmental Conference:

> In recognition of the Irish Government's special interest in Northern Ireland and of the extent to which issues of mutual concern arise in relation to Northern Ireland, there will be regular and frequent meetings of the Conference concerned with non-devolved Northern Ireland matters, on which the Irish Government may put

forward views and proposals. These meetings, to be co-chaired by the Minister for Foreign Affairs and the Secretary of State for Northern Ireland, would also deal with all-island and cross-border co-operation on non-devolved issues.

Co-operation within the framework of the Conference will include facilitation of co-operation in security matters. The Conference also will address, in particular, the areas of rights, justice, prisons and policing in Northern Ireland (unless and until responsibility is devolved to a Northern Ireland administration) and will intensify co-operation between the two Governments on the all-island or cross-border aspects of these matters. (https://www.britishirishcouncil.org/agreement-reached-multi-party-negotiations/strand-3-british-irish-council-and-intergovernmental)

As regards cross-border cooperation, the North–South Ministerial Council was established to manage various areas of cooperation. The North–South Ministerial Council's secretariat, based in Armagh, comprised civil servants from Northern Ireland and Ireland and was headed by one civil servant from the Department of Foreign Affairs and one Northern Irish civil servant from the OFMDFMNI. In response to unionist concerns, from a list of 140 areas, 6 areas were given designated cross-border joint bodies and 6 areas were identified as an area of cooperation, without joint bodies (Table 1).

The policy areas prioritised by the Good Friday Agreement and its new institutions are listed in Tables 2 and 3.

There was a strong EU dimension in the Good Friday Agreement's cross-border provisions, highlighted by the creation of the SEUPB, dedicated to managing cross-border EU Interreg funding projects, as well as Common Agricultural Policy (CAP) funding and the

Table 1. North–South implementation bodies (joint bodies)

Trade and Business Development Body (Intertrade Ireland)
Waterways Ireland
Food Safety Body (Safefood)
Foyle, Carlingford and Irish Lights Commission
The Language Body
SEUPB

Source: NSMC (2016), https://www.northsouthministerialcouncil.org/content/north-south-implementation-bodies

Table 2. Areas of cooperation

Agriculture: CAP issues, Animal and Plant Health Policy and Research Rural Development
Education: Education for children with special needs, educational under-achievement, teacher qualifications and school, youth and teacher exchanges
Environment: Environment protection, pollution, water quality management and waste management in a cross-border content
Health: Accident and emergency planning, co-operation on high technology equipment, cancer research and health promotion
Tourism: including Tourism Ireland: The promotion of the island of Ireland overseas as a tourist destination via the establishment of a new company, known as Tourism Ireland
Transport: Co-operation on a strategic road and rail infrastructure and public transport

Source: NSMC (2016), https://www.northsouthministerialcouncil.org/areas-of-cooperation

EU Peace packages to foster peace and reconciliation. In the next section, the impact of the Good Friday Agreement's cross-border and intergovernmental provisions is assessed.

The Impact of the Good Friday Agreement on Civil Service and Intergovernmental Cooperation

As regards the Good Friday Agreement's impact on intergovernmental cooperation, it is noteworthy that its policy formulation process reflected the evolution of close intergovernmental cooperation from 1985 onwards. There was strong joint executive control of the multi-party negotiating process, with a small team led by then prime ministers Bertie Ahern and Tony Blair. The process in the 1990s:

> sent a clear signal to unionists of the British intention of deepening cooperation with the Irish government and clear signal to republicans that they would not be able to bomb the British government into conceding on the principle of majoritarian consent for any change in status of Northern Ireland. (O'Duffy, 1999, p. 414)

Despite the Ulster Unionist Party (UUP) holding the balance of power in Westminster and using its leverage to bar Sinn Féin from negotiations until the IRA decommissioned its arms, British–Irish cooperation thrived (O'Duffy, 1999, p. 415). Thus, there is a high threshold to be reached in showing that the Good Friday Agreement *increased* intergovernmental cooperation after 1998.

After the Good Friday Agreement, both governments continued to cooperate closely. They responded unanimously to the decommissioning crisis in 2001, where the UUP and Democratic Unionist Party (DUP) argued that IRA decommissioning was not occurring. They also played a lead role in 2006 St Andrew's Agreement that amended the Good Friday Agreement and provided for policing reform. In 2016, both governments, represented by the Northern Ireland Secretary of State and the Irish Foreign Minister, led intensive talks to broker the Stormont House Agreement (https://www.dfa.ie/media/dfa/alldfawe bsitemedia/ourrolesandpolicies/northernireland/20151223-Stormont-House-Agreement—Document.pdf).

However, although generally cooperative, the relationship was not always smooth, for example:

> the limited capacity of the Irish government to influence its British counterpart was exposed in February 2000, when the British suspended the devolved institutions against the strong wishes of the Irish side. (Coakley, 2014, p. 81)

As regards the impact of peace and therefore implicitly the Good Friday Agreement's impact on British–Irish cooperation, there was evidence that the intergovernmental relationship was broadening to other areas. The 2011 visit of Queen Elizabeth was the first state visit by a UK monarch to Ireland since 1911. It was followed by a state visit by Irish President Higgins to London. These visits were followed in 2012 by the announcement of a new bilateral committee comprising heads of UK and Irish civil service departments, the Permanent Secretaries and Secretaries General Group (Coakley, 2014, p. 82), with a focus on developing further economic relations between Ireland and the UK. A system of annual bilateral meetings between both heads of government was also announced.

Both governments emphasised the strong cultural and economic connections between Ireland and Britain, with then prime minister David Cameron observing that Ireland was the UK's fifth biggest market, despite Ireland's small population size.

However, as regards the Good Friday Agreement's institutions for intergovernmental cooperation, there was no significant impact on British–Irish cooperation. As regards the British–Irish Intergovernmental Conference:

> The St Andrews Agreement of 2006 had the effect of reducing further the role of the Intergovernmental Conference. By providing for the creation of an inclusive Northern Ireland executive to manage major devolved areas … and for the devolution of control over policing … it removed responsibility over these areas from the Intergovernmental Conference and the momentum behind the conference seems to have evaporated. (Coakley, 2014, p. 81)

Thus, staff numbers fell in the British–Irish Intergovernmental Conference after 2007 and the UK side of the secretariat left the British–Irish Intergovernmental Conference office to move to Stormont (Coakley, 2014, p. 81). Unlike the formal underpinning of the 1985 Intergovernmental Conference, the British–Irish Intergovernmental Conference no longer holds regular and frequent meetings (Coakley, 2014, p. 81).

As regards the British–Irish Council, no UK prime minister has attended its meetings since Tony Blair and it is regarded by many as tangential. Thus, the Good Friday Agreement reflected a very strong intergovernmental relationship, but it did not increase intergovernmental cooperation and the focus on Northern Ireland was weaker from 2011, as the Northern Ireland Executive was in operation and Northern Ireland appeared to be stable. However, 'this informal British-Irish mode of implementing the Agreement and of adjudicating on its principles was, however, dependent on the states' prioritization of Northern Ireland' (Todd, 2015, para. 7).

However, the Good Friday Agreement did have an obvious impact on general civil service cross-border cooperation. Under the Good Friday Agreement, twelve departments are involved in cross-border cooperation, but in addition, the departments of Finance in Northern Ireland and Ireland and the Department of Foreign Affairs and Trade and the Department of the Taoiseach in Ireland and the OFMDNI in Northern Ireland are all involved in cross-border cooperation. The latter three departments are crucially involved in an on-going way in 'high' politics, agenda-setting and the content and outcomes of North–South Ministerial Council meetings. The 12 other departments are the 'sponsoring' departments for cross-border cooperation. Thus, the Good Friday Agreement has precipitated significant administrative changes in the Irish and Northern Irish civil service as Table 3 shows.

The creation of the North–South Ministerial Council provided for six sectoral meetings in designated areas with cross-border bodies and six meetings a year in areas of cooperation with no joint bodies. There are also two plenaries a year, attended by the First and Deputy First Ministers in Northern Ireland and the Irish Taoiseach. Irish and Northern Irish civil services were reorganised to help prepare for and engage with the North–South Ministerial Council. Most obviously, its secretariat in Armagh has approximately twelve civil servants form both jurisdictions, jointly headed by an Irish and Northern Irish senior civil servant. The North–South Ministerial Council also deals with areas of cooperation, such as agriculture and transport. Since 1999, each department of relevance to cross-border cooperation, the 'sponsoring department' has a coordinator within a unit, for example, the corporate unit,

Table 3. Institutional changes to Irish civil service and Northern Ireland Civil Service under Good Friday Agreement

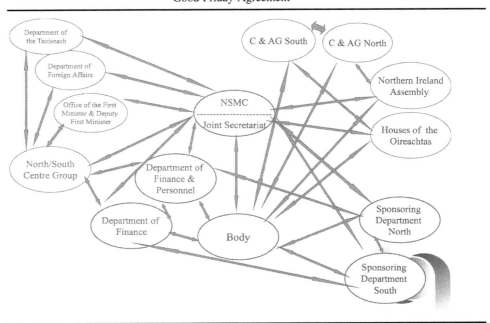

Source: Tourism Ireland, NSMC and civil service departments.

who collates information about issues for the North–South Ministerial Council's sectoral agenda and liaises with its Northern Irish counterpart to agree that agenda. These units liaise with civil servants in their departments across a range of issues, so a broad range of civil service actors become involved. The OFMDNI and the Department of Foreign Affairs then finalises the agenda before North–South Ministerial Council meetings occur. There is a large amount of interaction every four months as civil servants prepare for the North–South Ministerial Council sectoral and plenary meetings. As there are various sectors involved with different timelines, there is on-going cross-border civil service cooperation throughout the year.

The joint bodies and the agencies in charge of sectoral cooperation, for example, Tourism Ireland, feed into the sponsoring departments and must have their approval before embarking on new schemes. The agenda for the North–South Ministerial Council sectoral and plenary meetings is set by North–South units in each relevant department. For example, in agriculture, the corporate unit has a small number of staff responsible for collating a list of developments in agricultural cooperation from across the department and setting draft agendas for North–South Ministerial Council sectoral and plenary meetings. Therefore, the cross-dimension penetrates almost every unit in the department. Ultimately budgets are decided by the Irish Department of Finance and the OFMDNI and Finance in Northern Ireland. The agendas are finalised only with the approval of the OFMDNI and the Department of Foreign Affairs in Ireland. The cross-border arrangements are this subject to strong executive control in both jurisdictions, ensuring accountability and political consensus. For unionists, it was imperative that the Northern Irish Department of

Finance sign off on any new initiatives, ensuring that Irish governmental influence was not unfettered.

The total impact of the changes to civil service organisation in Northern Ireland and Ireland since the Good Friday Agreement cannot be underestimated. In all the sectors examined interviewees reported evidence of close cooperation both formally and informally. Apart from increased civil service cooperation in the areas covered by the Good Friday Agreement's provisions, civil servants also observed an increase in organic cooperation in areas where benefits from cooperation exist. For example in health, unionists supported the decision that Our Lady's Hospital Crumlin in Dublin would be the centre for paediatric heart surgery for the island, rather than having a centre in Belfast also. Similarly, there are cross-border emergency and ambulance services along the Irish border and a cross-border radiotherapy service in the North-West. In energy, Northern Ireland and Ireland are part of the Single Electricity Market initiative on the island, seeking to ensure the stability of supply form Scotland and to minimise prices. Therefore, civil servants in the energy and health sectors are in frequent contact and cooperate closely. Similarly, Tourism Ireland was set up to market Ireland as one area. Tourism Ireland's work has been commended, particularly in marketing to long-haul customers and numbers visiting the island from overseas have increased dramatically.

There are two striking features of the Good Friday Agreement's impact on civil service cooperation: firstly, the EU dimension is intertwined with cooperation in the Good Friday Agreement. Secondly, while the original basis of civil service cooperation stemmed from the Good Friday Agreement's list of areas of cooperation and areas where joint bodies existed, gradually civil service cooperation became more organic and developed in areas where common pragmatic interests existed, for example, in health, energy and telecommunications, not mentioned in the Good Friday Agreement. In the next section, the significance of the EU dimension is assessed, before assessing the impact of Brexit on intergovernmental and cross-border civil service cooperation.

The EU and Cooperation

One of the key cross-border bodies was the SEUPB. The SEUPB is responsible for managing all EU funding and is therefore responsible for administering Interreg to cover cooperation with Ireland, Northern Ireland and Western Scotland. For 2014–2020, the European Regional Development Fund (ERDF) contribution to the Programme is €240 m (85%) (SEUPB, 2014). In addition €43 m (15%) will come from match-funding, raising the total value of the Programme to €283 m (SEUPB, 2014). The key priorities funded by Interreg are environment, transport, public health care and research and innovation. On one level, Interreg is relevant to various civil service departments. However, its relatively small budget as a proportion of both EU funding and national expenditure and the role of the SEUPB as well as its grassroot/community level focus mean that there was not much evidence of its impact on wider civil service cooperation. It was of more relevance to the work of the NSMC Secretariat in Armagh. It is also noteworthy that the amount of funding received in total from the EU is significantly smaller than that for Northern Ireland, as Table 4 shows.

Cooperation revolves around civil servants learning about how an EU policy may affect them from other civil servants, or it involves agreeing on implementing a policy that has cross-border dimensions, for example, soil quality along the Irish border. Thus, civil

Table 4. Northern Ireland Structural Funds and CAP allocation 2014–2020 (million euro)

ERDF	308
European Social Fund Programme	183
INTERREG VA	240
PEACE IV	229
European Fisheries and Maritime Fund	24
Rural Development Programme (CAP Pillar 2)	227
CAP Pillar 111	2,299 million

Source: Northern Ireland Select Committee: Northern Ireland Structural Funds and CAP allocation 2014–2020, paragraph 8.

service cooperation developed organically as regards the EU also, where there was a perceived need to share lessons and briefings on EU policies. As Hayward and Murphy (2018) show in this volume, the EU provided a valuable context for cross-border cooperation that may be difficult to replace in the absence of political will.

However, there were some qualifications to the success of Northern Irish–Irish civil service cooperation in the twenty-first century and evidence that rather than such cooperation overcoming ethnic divides, ethnic conflict has constrained administrative dynamism, even with elite level policy leadership from British and Irish governments. Firstly, the power-sharing system in Northern Ireland, whereby policy was decided by consensus made it more difficult for Northern Irish civil servants to innovate. Their dynamism was also impeded, as any innovation or change must be approved by the DUP and Sinn Féin and in a post-conflict situation, seemingly innocuous changes can be politically sensitive. Similarly, the degree of enthusiasm for cross-border cooperation depended on whether a Sinn Féin, or Unionist Minister holds the brief for that policy. A stronger case must be made for the economic logic of a cross-border endeavour to unionist ministers. Civil servants on both sides of the border found that once there was an evidence-based logic of cross-border cooperation in a certain area, all parties usually agree, but the process was painstaking, from setting dates for North–South Ministerial Council meetings, to the wording of its agenda items. Obviously, the current suspension of the Northern Ireland executive hinders administrative cooperation and precludes meetings.

A second qualification is that all civil servants observed that there were areas where each jurisdiction has conflicts of interest—where they compete. Although, there was far less evidence of competitive approaches hindering cross-border cooperation in Ireland, than in the early 1990s, there are still areas where each jurisdiction. For example, although Tourism Ireland has been highly successful, Bord Fáilte and the Northern Irish Tourist Board continue to exist and their brief is to market each jurisdiction. Thus, there have been issues raised about the marketing of the Giant's Causeway in Northern Ireland as 'Irish', when it is not located in the Irish state and also an awareness that for short-break visitors, Dublin and Belfast do compete, as do other Northern Irish and Irish cities. Another key example of competition is in inward investment. Specifically, Northern Ireland has received a guarantee from the UK government that its corporation tax will be lowered, to help it attract overseas investment and compete with Ireland's lower corporation tax rate. In broad terms, Northern Ireland, Ireland are competitors and while there is evidence of increased civil service cooperation, there are large areas where competition prevails.

Finally, the informality that characterises cooperation could imply that cooperation could fall prey to new conditions, or increased competition in the future. As regards cross-border cooperation, clearly the Good Friday Agreement institutionalises cross-border cooperation and the British–Irish Council and Intergovernmental Conference institutionalise limited intergovernmental cooperation. The bilateral London-Dublin summit idea, since 2012, also institutionalises British–Irish intergovernmental cooperation. However, these institutions have not flourished in the way that Hume may have envisaged and British–Irish formalised cooperation is more limited than cross-border cooperation. In addition, Brexit has created significant strains, as the next section shows.

Brexit and the Intergovernmental and Cross-Border Civil Service Relationship

The Brexit referendum result returned 56% of Northern Irish voters voting to remain, with the DUP eventually supporting a Leave vote, but the UUP, Sinn Féin and the SDLP and Alliance supporting Remain. The shock of Brexit impacted negatively on all civil service departments across the UK and Ireland. The sources of potential friction are multifaceted (Tannam, 2017a):

- A majority of voters in Northern Ireland, with a dominant nationalist component, voted to remain in the EU and under the terms of the Good Friday Agreement and the basis of British–Irish intergovernmentalism, the Irish government is obliged to protect their interests in the face of the UK government exiting the EU. The UK government is obliged not to take sides in undermining nationalist interests-both are meant to be honest brokers and guarantors of the Agreement.
- Northern Irish support for Remain led Sinn Féin to call for a poll on Irish unity, automatically calling into question the Good Friday Agreement.
- As McCall argues in this volume, Brexit immediately created dilemmas about securitisation of the border and how to avoid it (McCall, 2018). The apparently irreconcilable aims of maintaining a soft border (UK and Irish governments' preferences) and limiting freedom of movement (the UK government's aims) and the absence of detail in the UK government's position paper on Brexit and Northern Ireland, have meant that the Irish government became increasingly frustrated at UK governmental behaviour.
- Once Article 50 was triggered in March 2017, the Irish government as part of the 27 member state EU negotiating team and the UK government were not on the same side, for the first time in decades. The Irish government was not free to bargain unilaterally with the UK, even if the UK requested it. Thus, both governments could not share information in the way they once did. The European Council's decision that the negotiations would occur in three stages, not simultaneously and that substantial progress must be made in stage one, dealing with the Irish border, citizens' rights and the 'divorce' bill to be paid by the UK, reflected intensive lobbying by Irish officials from September 2016, to ensure that the UK government would not link the border issue to gaining concessions in a trade deal. UK and Irish government interests and preferences were already diverging. Similarly, the EU stance that it is not its responsibility to solve the Irish border issue, because it is the UK's responsibility, reflected the Irish government's position and was at odds with UK preferences.
- More generally, Brexit means that the Irish government has lost a powerful ally with whom it shared many common interests in the EU. Instead, it is faced with conflicts of

interest emerging from economic conflicts, for example, fisheries. 'Brexit unilaterally and arbitrarily breaks these conditions of Irish-British interdependence' (Gillespie, 2017).

Yet, Northern Ireland did not feature in the UK Brexit campaign, either in most media accounts, or among politicians. Complacency about Northern Ireland was evident when David Cameron announced that there would be a referendum on Brexit. Given the EU dimension to the Good Friday Agreement and the high sensitivity of the Irish border in a post-conflict context and in the relatively early stages of the border 'normalising', the decision was an obvious destabilising influence for Northern Ireland. Although, this weak prioritisation can be explained by Cameron's confidence that the 'Remain' side would win, the announcement created immediate divisions in Northern Ireland, with the DUP eventually supporting 'Leave' and the UUP, Sinn Féin and the SDLP and Alliance supporting Remain.

Despite the strong intergovernmental relationship, it was telling that even before the referendum result, an advisor to David Cameron observed that when he attempted to include Northern Ireland as an issue in the campaign, emphasising that its sensitivities must be addressed, there was no appetite to do so, as Northern Ireland was not a significant issue for the English electorate (O'Toole, 2017). The timing of the Brexit referendum to coincide with Assembly election campaign in Northern Ireland, despite Northern Irish party pleas to avoid such a clash, also highlighted the limits of intergovernmental cooperation. In contrast to the intergovernmental logic that any issues of relevance to Northern Ireland and Ireland that could be destabilising should be discussed with the Irish government and joint decision reached, the decision to have a Brexit referendum was clearly a domestic political strategy by David Cameron to solidify his base and as such there was no Irish governmental advice, or input.

The Irish government stressed that the Brexit issue was the UK's sovereign right and it was not in a position to request that the referendum date be changed. Similarly, while Irish officials were instructed by the Irish government to prepare various scenarios of the implications of Brexit for the Irish border and cooperation, depending on the Brexit result and the final EU-UK deal that might occur, the UK government did not plan. Again, according to intergovernmental logic, joint planning should have occurred, with information exchange and joint problem-solving for each scenario, rather than the Irish government's unilateral attempt to plan.

At the time of writing, two key periods can be identified in the intergovernmental relationship: June to April 2017 and April 2017 to March 2018. Both periods are marked by intensive Irish diplomatic and political lobbying of EU member states in their capital cities, in Brussels and Strasbourg and by UK governmental disarray and chaos that damaged its management of Brexit. In the first period, the rhetoric of both UK and Irish governments was to affirm the importance of Northern Ireland's stability and the British–Irish, with various UK government politicians using phrases such as 'frictionless border' and 'no return to the borders of the past' (*The Guardian*, July 26, 2016).

Given the role of EU funding in Strand 2 of the Good Friday Agreement and the assumption of EU membership, when the Good Friday Agreement was signed, an immediate question mark was whether it would need amendment, whether a new bilateral UK–Irish Treaty was required to protect it (House of Lords, 2016), or at worst, whether its existence was in jeopardy (Tonge, 2016). Sinn Féin's calls for a border poll added to tensions. These calls were followed quickly by Fianna Fail also calling for a poll and preparing a road map for Irish in unification (*Irish Times*, 2017a). The UK governmental response again was that there would be no return to the borders of the past and that the Good Friday Agreement would not be undermined. The Irish government emphasised the North–South Ministerial Council as the means 'to forge a common approach to Brexit related issues' and in July 2016, it agreed to work together to fully analyse the sectoral implications of Brexit for Ireland, North and South (Department of Taoiseach, 2017a).

As the shock of the Brexit referendum was absorbed, the Irish response was to limit damage and to lobby EU and member state officials vigorously to ensure that Northern Ireland would be prioritised in the forthcoming Brexit negotiations. Four issues emerged in the Irish government's position paper (Department of Taoiseach, 2017a):

- To avoid a hard border, that is a wish to ensure that freedom of movement, legally enshrined by the 1948 bilateral Common Travel Area Agreement between Ireland and the UK
- To preserve freedom of movement of trade
- To protect Irish citizen's rights in the UK
- To protect the Good Friday Agreement.

In December 2016, the UK prime minister's white paper on Brexit included preserving the Common Travel Area as a priority (UK Government, 2017) and was welcomed by the Irish prime minister. The January 31 summit between May and Kenny in Dublin used similar terms, but as commentators noted did not specify how such an outcome could be achieved (*Irish Times*, 2017b).

As regards the EU dimension to the Good Friday Agreement, the Irish government's approach was that the Agreement's appendix provided for amendment and that amendment had occurred at various times, for example in the 2006 St Andrew's Agreement, so amendment to take account of Brexit was not necessarily drastic and did not require a new Treaty. As regards a border poll the Irish government rejected the idea, but the new Minister for Foreign Affairs reiterated that Fine Gael supported Irish unification, but only with the consent of nationalists and unionists. Sinn Féin also withdrew from a dramatic border poll call and referred to Irish unification as a 'strategy' (*Irish Times*, 2017c).

The EU recognised the sensitivity of Northern Ireland, following intensive Irish diplomatic lobbying and included Northern Ireland as 1 of the 3 priorities (the others being the Brexit 'bill' and citizens' rights) where the 27 EU states must agree that there was substantial progress, before the Brexit negotiations could move to discussing trade issues. The EU also made a special declaration that if in the future a majority voted for Irish unification, Northern Ireland would automatically gain re-entry to the EU (Reuters, 2017). It stated its willingness to reach a special arrangement for Northern Ireland's border and the Council President; Donald Tusk stated in his invitation letter to the Council that 'in order to protect the peace and reconciliation process described by the Good Friday Agreement, we should aim to avoid a hard border between the Republic of Ireland and Northern Ireland' (European Council, 2017).

From April 2017 to March 2018, the UK government's continued absence of clarity about its preferences for the future trade relationship and its proposal for Northern Ireland and the border issue, led to increased tensions in the intergovernmental relationship. An Irish governmental strategy to adopt a tougher stance gradually developed. Thus, in

April 2017, the then Irish Minister for Foreign Affairs and Trade, Charlie O'Flanagan criticised the UK government for not engaging adequately with the Irish government over its Brexit plans and heavily criticised Theresa May's statement that no (Brexit) deal was better than a bad deal (*Irish Times*, 2016a).

The problem was exacerbated by the return of a weak Tory government after the June 2017 election and the new government's confidence and supply agreement with the DUP cast an immediate doubt over whether the UK government could still perform its role as an honest broker under the Good Friday Agreement. The new Taoiseach Leo Vardakar and the new Irish Minister for Foreign Affairs took an increasingly hard line. He consistently emphasised that Brexit created problems of UK making and that it was up to the UK, not the Irish government to propose solutions (Department of Taoiseach, 2017a).

In addition, the UK government's long-awaited position paper on Brexit and Northern Ireland in September 2016 appeared to link resolving the border issue to reaching a trade agreement with the EU, rather than making progress on the Northern Ireland first and then moving to trade, as instructed by the EU and the Irish government. Although the UK government in the paper supported the Good Friday Agreement and opposed a customs border, the then Irish Minister for Foreign Affairs, Simon Coveney, warned that Northern Ireland must not be a pawn in the Brexit negotiations amid fears that the UK government was attempting to use the Northern Ireland border issue to gain the perks of an EU customs union, without the obligations.

The Irish government's decision to use megaphone diplomacy and engage in brinkmanship was risky as it marked a major departure from a joint British–Irish strategy, devised in the mid-1980s. It resisted the consensual language of intergovernmental cooperation and of the Good Friday Agreement and it reverted to zero-sum characterisations of Brexit and the border issue, whereby the issue was not a problem to be solved jointly in bilateral meetings before Article 50 was triggered, but was a UK problem—'the UK's fault'. Thus, in March 2018, the EU–UK's draft withdrawal agreement contained a protocol on Northern Ireland, stating that if no other satisfactory arrangement was reached to protect a soft border, then a single market and custom union would be provided for on the island for all areas deemed necessary for the functioning of the cross-border provisions of the Good Friday Agreement.

The Irish governmental strategy worked because it correctly calculated that it could not rely on the UK government to resolve the border issue satisfactorily unless it played tough (Tannam, 2017b). Indeed, even a week before the the December text that prioritised the border issue and the Good Friday Agreement, there were UK media commentaries, apparently drawn from UK Cabinet ministers, that once the divorce bill was agreed, the EU would soon cave in on the border issue and there were reports that UK officials were adopting a strategy of divide and conquer in the EU, in the hope that the Irish border issue would not be an obstacle moving to trade talks. In addition, there were various reports that the Irish government was 'playing tough' about the border because it was bowing to Sinn Féin, a view echoed publicly by the Brexit Secretary David Davis on the 20th anniversary of the Good Friday Agreement (*The Times*, 2018).

Any examination of the British–Irish intergovernmental relationship from 2016 to 2018 cannot but reveal the large negative change in the dynamics of that relationship, compared to the previous thirty years and the minimal impact of the Good Friday Agreement's executive and consultative institutions in mitigating that change. 'Overall, by 2018, Brexit had created strains in the bilateral relationship'. The most optimistic scenario was that once the negotiations were completed, the formerly positive relationship would be revived.

The rhetoric was part of a short-term strategy during the Brexit negotiations. For example, the Irish Minister for Foreign Affairs mentioned that a new bilateral agreement could be signed after Brexit (Coveney, 2018, January 31).

Impact of Brexit on Civil Service Cross-Border Cooperation

Immediately after the decision to hold a Brexit referendum was announced, Irish civil departments began setting out various scenarios, according to the Brexit result and various Brexit negotiating outcomes (Department of Taoiseach, 2016). The administrative burden multiplied after the Brexit result and involved close cooperation with counterparts in the Northern Ireland Civil Service. For example, the North–South Ministerial Council commissioned an audit of the sectors most affected by Brexit, involving significant cross-border civil service cooperation Joint Communique, July 4, 2016. It pledged to 'ensure that Northern Ireland's interests are protected and advanced and the benefits of North/South cooperation are fully recognised in any new arrangements which emerge' (North–South Ministerial Council Joint Communique, 7 July 2016). The Loughs Agency in conjunction with the relevant environmental civil service departments undertook an initial assessment of Brexit's impact (North–South Ministerial Council, Joint Communique, 14 September 2016). Both Irish and Northern Irish representatives agreed that the North–South Ministerial Council could provide a useful forum for ongoing discussion (North–South Ministerial Council Joint Communique, 4 July 2016), thereby necessitating civil service cooperation through the North–South Ministerial Council Secretariat. However, the suspension of the Executive following DUP-Sinn Féin disagreements meant that the North–South Ministerial Council ceased to operate for the duration of the suspension. Civil service informal contacts continued in key economic sectors. Ironically, in the short term at least, Brexit has created common cross-border interests, as both jurisdictions aim to minimise costs of Brexit to their economies and also aim to avoid destabilising effects politically.

After the Brexit referendum, the Irish government restructured the roles of the Department of Taoiseach and the Department of Foreign Affairs in the aftermath of the referendum, creating a coordinating Brexit committee and recognising that the Minster for Foreign Affairs was the de facto Brexit minister also, under the Taoiseach's leadership. (Department of Taoiseach, 2017b). The Department of the Taoiseach's International, EU and Northern Ireland Division 'support and advise the Taoiseach in all his engagement on International, EU and Northern Ireland Affairs' and 'plays a significant role in ensuring a coordinated approach' to all issues arising from Brexit (Department of Taoiseach, 2017c).

The Department of Foreign Affairs launched a vast lobbying exercise across national capitals, in the EU and in London to ensure that Northern Ireland would be a priority issue and it continued to lobby throughout 2017. The Taoiseach also announced that the size of the diplomatic corps would be increased substantially.

However, the elephant in the room from January 2017 was the collapse of the Northern Ireland Executive. Although the reasons for the collapse are complex (O'Leary, 2018) and it was not directly caused by Brexit, its collapse hinders cross-border dynamism and civil service cooperation and it further exacerbates Brexit's negative impacts. In addition, Brexit's effect on Irish civil service cooperation with Whitehall was negative.

In response to the Brexit referendum result, the UK government set up the Department for Exiting the EU (DexEU), comprising some Cabinet Office staff as well as former staff who were asked to return. Although initial upheaval was expected, as the UK government faced the mammoth task of negotiating its exit from the EU, as well as its future relationship, it was clear that the upheaval was lasting beyond the preliminary stages, exacerbated by domestic UK politics and a weak Conservative government. Thus, British–Irish communication was less than might be expected. Some staff who had been key contacts had been moved to DEXEU, so contacts had to be rebuilt. Fundamentally, the UK administration was immediately faced with a huge policy agenda and prioritising British–Irish relations was difficult to ensure. In other words, the infrequency of communication between Irish and UK government officials, noted by Irish Minister O'Flanagan, affected some aspects of civil service cooperation. Writing in December 2017, the Permanent had not met in over a year. However, there is a distinction between high- level communication and technical talks. Thus, Irish and UK civil servants in the relevant departments communicated more frequently in areas of social policy such as pensions and social welfare, for example.

Apart from the sheer burden of work leading to fears that the UK government was not prioritising Northern Ireland, or UK–Irish relations, once the first stage of the Brexit negotiations began, Ireland was part of the EU negotiating team and although both the UK government and the Irish government shared Northern Ireland as a common interest, albeit more strongly prioritised by the Irish government, Irish diplomats was no longer in a position to defend UK interests, or to negotiate any separate agreement with UK diplomats, even if the latter Foreign and Cabinet office staff had the resources and time to do so. Thus automatically, the diplomatic relationship altered. In addition, 'as open economically liberal states, Ireland and the UK have … found themselves on the same side' in various trade, tax and financial matters (*Irish Times*, October 19, 2016b), Brexit removed these common bargaining interests and placed pressure on the Irish government and its diplomats to build new alliances within the EU.

Conclusion

In 2016, when the proposal for this special edition was being prepared, this author was not alone in envisaging a very different celebration of the 20th anniversary of the Good Friday Agreement. Brexit has created an unprecedented set of challenges to policy makers and bureaucrats on both sides of the Irish sea. In assessing the intergovernmental and cross-border administrative relationships, there are some clear observations, but as this volume went to press, only a tentative analysis is possible.

The Good Friday Agreement and peace both reflected and caused increased bilateral and cross-border administrative cooperation. Relationships were strained and curtailed until the 1980s. Gradually, the intergovernmental relationship improved and was at the basis of the peace process in the 1990s. Civil service cross-border cooperation was slower to develop, but in the aftermath of the Good Friday Agreement, it too evolved, albeit with some departments more involved than others and with fluctuations depending on the status of the Northern Ireland Executive.

Civil service cooperation was politically driven by British and Irish governments and not functionalist in origin. Despite the EU's economic incentives for cooperation in the 1990s and the existence of apparent common economic interests as peripheral regions in the Single Market, civil service departments in Northern Ireland and Ireland with economic policy responsibilities generally behaved as competitors, or ignored each other, until the Good Friday Agreement. The Agreement's institutional provisions for administrative cooperation led to a new dynamism in the relationship. Stemming from that dynamism there was evidence of more organic cooperation by 2018.

As regards intergovernmental cooperation, rather than the Good Friday Agreement causing increased intergovernmental cooperation, it reflected that cooperation. The Agreement's East-West institutions did not increase levels of cooperation and they lacked dynamism, partially because peace made them see less necessary. However, the broader British-Irish intergovernmental relationship apparently flourished with flagship events such as Queen Elizabeth's visit to Ireland in 2011.

Finally, Brexit referendum has created large strains in the relationship, reflected in the rhetoric of both governments and the depiction of the Irish government in some UK media accounts, as well as in the relatively infrequent incidence of meetings between prime ministers. As regards civil service cooperation, there is still strong cooperation at the technical level in areas such as social policy and pensions. Cooperation would be expected to be strong in the security and health policy areas also. There is also on-going communication between Irish and British civil servants at the coalface of the Brexit negotiations, for example the lead official dealing with Brexit in the Irish Department of Taoiseach and his UK counterpart. However, the longer-term impact of Brexit on cross-border civil service relations is not clear. Much depends on the final deal and areas such as energy, food safety and animal health will still require cooperation, even if the UK is not in the Customs Union. If the Northern Ireland Executive is not restored, the North-South Ministerial Council will obviously fail to deliver further cooperation.

An analysis of the underlying causes of weakness in the British-Irish relationship is necessarily tentative given the short-time frame. As predicted by Jennifer Todd (Todd, 2015), the weakness in implementing Strand 3 of the Good Friday Agreement in a dynamic way from 1998 onwards meant that before and immediately after the Brexit referendum, there was no embedded bilateral institutional framework that legally obliged both governments to meet.

Both the Brexit campaign itself and the UK government's treatment of the border issue imply that despite the close relationship of the 1990s and the strategy of the 1980s, the 3 strands approach of the Agreement and the primacy of bilateral cooperation was never as fully embedded in UK elite circles. Possibly, the problem was accentuated with a Conservative government is in power, but nor did the Labour Party appear to prioritise Northern Ireland in its Brexit campaign and nor is its track record historically any better than that of the Conservative Party.

The Irish government's bargaining strategy can be explained by its awareness that the UK government was not prioritising Northern Ireland and by perceptions that not only that, the UK government could seek to use the border issue to seek a satisfactory trade deal in phase two of the Brexit negotiations, unless agreement was reached on the border issue before trade talks began. In this way, both governments did not share a common first preference in the Brexit negotiations. The UK government's first preference ostensibly was to leave the Customs Union and Single Market with a trade deal to its satisfaction. The Irish government's first preference was to protect a soft border and the Good Friday Agreement.

As the negotiations progressed, both sets of preferences became increasingly conflictual. Although the UK government appeared to share the interest of protecting a soft border in Northern Ireland, this priority appeared to rank more lowly on its list of aims than for the Irish government and it appeared that the UK government was willing to forsake it in return for its higher priority - trade. In contrast to the 1980s and 1990s, when there were various conflicts of interest, but the core common interest of stemming paramilitary violence was shared equally by both governments (even if there were disagreements about the means to do so), the Brexit negotiations increasingly revealed the absence of a shared core priority.

Also unlike the 1980s and 1990s, the Irish government was not as free to initiate bilateral bargaining to achieve a solution, especially once Article 50 was triggered. Formally, the Irish government as part of the EU was not as free to engage in structured formalised bilateral negotiations with the UK government. Apart from this constraint, the existence of conflicting priorities implied that adequate levels of trust did not exist in the first place to engage in sustained bilateral negotiations: UK and Irish awareness of each other's intense preferences opened each side up to the possibility of being exploited. In addition the while the Brexit negotiations also showed the coherence of the Irish government's aims and coherence, the lack of clarity from the UK government and its various contradictory statements made it difficult to enter into a rational bargaining process at all. In short, Brexit dramatically altered the cost-benefit analysis of the bilateral bargaining relationship and created a complex, if not confusing bargaining context.

Writing in May 2018, it is unclear whether current bilateral strains reflect a combination of a short-term strategy and a muddling through approach (in the UK case) that will end once the EU and the Irish government are satisfied that a soft border and the Good Friday Agreement are protected legally. The optimistic scenario is that if and when Brexit is agreed efforts will be made to rebuild relations and greater use of bilateral institutions will occur. The pessimistic scenario is that sufficient political will is needed not just to create institutions, but to maximise their potential. Given the UK's post-Brexit agenda, it is possible that there will be only limited political will to invest time in the British-Irish relationship. However, the implications of Brexit for Northern Ireland's constitutional future (see O'Leary, 2018), as well as its economic challenges (Bradley, 2018) and its potential to destabilise Northern Ireland mean that a robust institutional response is as necessary now as it was in the 1980s.

Acknowledgements

The author is grateful to The Long Room Hub, Trinity College Dublin's Institute for Research in the Arts and Humanities, for funding to conduct research for this article.

Funding

Trinity Long Room Hub for the Arts and Humanities partially funded field research for this article.

References

Arthur, P. (2000). *Special relationships*. Belfast: Blackstaff Press.

Bradley, J. (2018). The Irish-Northern Irish economic relationship: The Belfast Agreement, UK devolution and the EU. *Ethnopolitics*. doi:10.1080/17449057.2018.1472423

Coakley, J. (2014). British Irish institutional structures: Towards a new relationship. *Irish Political Studies*, 29(1), 76–97.

Coveney, S. (2018, January 31). The British-Irish relationship: Past, present and future. *Speech to Chatham House London*. Retrieved from https://www.chathamhouse.org/event/british-irish-relationship-past-present-and-future.

Department of Taoiseach. (2017a). Retrieved from http://www.taoiseach.gov.ie/eng/News/Taoiseach's_Speeches/Statement_by_the_Taoiseach_Statements_on_Northern_Ireland_Dail_Eireann_17_January_2017.html

Department of Taoiseach. (2017b). *Structure of the Department of Taoiseach, 2017.* Retrieved from http://www.taoiseach.gov.ie/eng/Work_Of_The_Department/Organisation%20Chart/)

Department of Taoiseach. (2017c). Retrieved from http://www.taoiseach.gov.ie/DOT/eng/Work_Of_The_Department/International_European_Union_and_Northern_Ireland_Division/International_European_Union_and_Northern_Ireland_Division.html)

Department of the Taoiseach. (2016). Retrieved from http://www.taoiseach.gov.ie/eng/News/Taoiseach's_Speeches/Statement_in_the_Dail_on_the_UK_EU_Referendum_Result_by_the_Taoiseach_Mr_Enda_Kenny_TD_Monday_27_June_2016.htm

European Council. (2017, December 15). *Guideline.* http://www.consilium.europa.eu/media/32236/15-euco-art50-guidelines-en.pdf

Ferriter, D. (2005). *The transformation of Ireland 1900–2000.* London: Profile Books.

Gillespie, P. (2017, December 23). Brexit unilaterally and arbitrarily breaks these conditions of Irish-British interdependence. *Irish Times.* Retrieved from https://www.irishtimes.com/opinion/brexit-breaks-delicate-interdependence-between-ireland-and-uk-1.3335532

Guardian. (2016, July 26). *Brexit will not threaten your stability and peace, May Northern Ireland's leaders.*

Haas, E. (1958). *The uniting of Europe.* Stanford: Stanford University Press.

Hayward, K., & Murphy, M. C. (2018). The EU's influence on the peace process and agreement in Northern Ireland in light of Brexit. *Ethnopolitics.* doi:10.1080/17449057.2018.1472426

House of Lords. (2016). *Brexit: UK-Irish relations.* Retrieved from https://publications.parliament.uk/pa/ld201617/ldselect/ldeucom/76/76.pdf

Irish Times. (2016a, December 24). Retrieved from http://www.irishtimes.com/news/politics/minister-criticises-british-government-over-brexit-strategy-1.2916819

Irish Times. (2016b, October 19). *Huge challenges loom as state to lose key EU ally.*

Irish Times. (2017a, March 13). *Fianna fail to publish roadmap for a United Ireland.*

Irish Times. (2017b, January 31). *Seamless, frictionless … meaningless: Leaders avoid rubbing each other up the wrong way.*

Irish Times. (2017c, August 9). Retrieved from https://www.irishtimes.com/news/politics/sinn-féin-would-want-irish-unification-plan-in-any-government-deal-1.3181316

McCall, C. (2018). Brexit, bordering and people on the Island of Ireland. *Ethnopolitics.* doi:10.1080/17449057.2018.1472425

McColgan, J. (1981). Partition and Irish Administration 1920–22. *Administration, 28,* 147–183.

Mitrany, D. (1975). *A working peace system.*

NSMC. (2016). Retrieved from https://www.northsouthministerialcouncil.org/areas-of-cooperation

NSMC Joint Communique. (2016a, July 4). 22nd Plenary Meeting. Retrieved from https://www.northsouthministerialcouncil.org/sites/northsouthministerialcouncil.org/files/publications/Plenary%20Joint%20Communique%20-%20English%20-%2004%20Jul-16.pdf

NSMC Joint Communique. (2016b, July 7). North–South Ministerial Council SEUPB Joint Communique, 7 July. Retrieved from https://www.northsouthministerialcouncil.org/publications/seupb-joint-communique-7-july-2016

NSMC Joint Communique. (2016c, September 14). North–South Ministerial Council Joint Communique, 2016. Retrieved from https://www.northsouthministerialcouncil.org/publications/environment-joint-communique-14-september-2016

O'Duffy, B. (1999). British and Irish conflict regulation from Sunningdale to Belfast. Part I: Tracing the status of contesting sovereigns, 1968–1974. *Nations and Nationalism, 5*(4), 523–542.

O'Leary, B. (2018). Postscript: New British questions or *2019 and all that! Ethnopolitics.* doi:10.1080/17449057.2018.1473115

O'Leary, B., & McGarry, J. (1993). *The politics of antagonism: Understanding Northern Ireland.* London: Athlone.

O'Leary, C., Elliott, S., & Wilford, R. (1988). *The Northern Ireland Assembly, 1982-86, a constitutional experiment.* London: Hurst.

O'Toole, M. (2017). Ireland an afterthought during brexit campaign when I was Cameron adviser. *Irish Times,* October 4. Retrieved from https://www.irishtimes.com/opinion/ireland-an-afterthought-during-brexit-campaign-when-i-was-cameron-adviser-1.3242732

Reuters. (2017, April 28). Retrieved from http://www.reuters.com/article/us-britain-eu-ireland-idUSKBN17U12W

SEUPB. (2014). Retrieved from http://www.seupb.eu/Libraries/INTERREG_VA_Programme_Guidance/IVA_CitizensSummary_English_Version3.sflb.ashx

Tannam, E. (1999). *Cross-border cooperation in Ireland and Northern Ireland Basingstoke.* Dublin: Macmillan.

Tannam, E. (2017a). *Submission to UK Government*, Foreign Affairs Committee.

Tannam, E. (2017b). Retrieved from http://blogs.lse.ac.uk/brexit/2017/12/05/a-high-risk-game-of-chicken-is-being-played-over-the-irish-border/)

The Times. (2018, April 10). Retrieved from https://www.thetimes.co.uk/article/davis-accuses-irish-leader-of-bowing-to-sinn-fein-pressure-9km6tsv6w

Todd, J. (2015). The vulnerability of the Northern Ireland settlement: British Irish relations, political crisis and Brexit. *Études irlandaises*, 40(2), 61–73.

Tonge, J. (2016). The impact of withdrawal from the European Union upon Northern Ireland. *The Political Quarterly*, *87*(3), 338–342.

UK Government. (2017). *The government's negotiating objectives for exiting the EU: PM*. Retrieved from https://www.gov.uk/government/speeches/the-governments-negotiating-objectives-for-exiting-the-eu-pm-speech

The Irish–Northern Irish Economic Relationship: The Belfast Agreement, UK Devolution and the EU

JOHN BRADLEY

ABSTRACT The 20th anniversary of the signing of the Belfast Agreement comes at a time of great discord, both within Northern Ireland (where, at the time of writing, the power-sharing executive is suspended) and between the UK and the EU (where March 2019 is the date set for Brexit). Given the close political and economic relationships between Ireland and the UK, and the need for both states to ensure sustained prosperity within Northern Ireland to assist the maintenance of peace, any evaluation of the Agreement needs to be placed in the wider context of the island of Ireland and Britain and not just focused on Northern Ireland. The main economic aspects of the Agreement are summarised, as well as the historical background to island economic strategy and the operation of the Agreement itself, the disruptive role played by Brexit is assessed and some suggestions are made about what might be needed to deal with its outcome.

Introduction

Given the fraught political climate of the 1990s, it is understandable that economic and business questions were not regarded as central to the search for peace and were largely absent from the table during the Agreement negotiations. It was only in the concluding stages, when a political breakthrough finally seemed within grasp, that a hurried effort was made to introduce measures that would serve to promote cross-border trade, business cooperation and other issues of an economic or socio-economic kind.[1]

In examining the economic impact of the Agreement, it is essential to understand the historical island context in which it is embedded. To ignore this context risks distorting any interpretation of the operation of the Agreement as well as the importance of Brexit to the island economy. In Section 1, the main provisions for cross-border and East–West cooperation under the Belfast Agreement are outlined, namely Strands 2 and 3 of the Agreement. In Section 2, some possible explanations are provided for the relegation of economic issues to the sidelines leading up to the period of the negotiation of the Agreement. Section 3 considers the manner in which the economic side of the Agreement played out over the past two decades. In Section 4, the potentially corrosive interaction of the evolution of the island economy under the Agreement in the disruptive context of Brexit is examined. Section 5 concludes with an exploration of the likely consequences and how this might affect any future of the Belfast Agreement.

Economic Aspects of the Belfast Agreement

The Belfast Agreement held out prospects of economic and business recovery and modernisation to the strife-torn region of Northern Ireland. However, there were different views of how best to advance economic recovery. Although their strategic views were not always expressed clearly and unambiguously, in general the Unionist/Loyalist parties favoured remaining as a regional economy of the UK; feared that any loosening of links with Britain would endanger the constitutional status of Northern Ireland; and tended to regard North–South links to Ireland as potentially subversive to what they perceived as their threatened 'Britishness' (Trimble, 1998). The Nationalist/Republican parties, on the other hand, had more outward-looking, global perspectives and favoured building on North–South links in order to reproduce in Northern Ireland the Irish model of development led by high technology foreign direct investment (Tannam, 1999). The existence of such divergent views did not augur well for the economic outcome of the talks that culminated in 1998 with the Belfast Agreement. The Agreement dealt with both economic governance in Northern Ireland under Strand 1 and with cross-border and East–West economic relationships, under Strands 2 and 3.

Strand 1

Economic governance in Northern Ireland is provided for under Strand 1 of the Agreement, dealing with the internal political governance of Northern Ireland. Northern Ireland is both a peripheral regional economy within the UK as well as being a geographical region of the island of Ireland. Although it enjoyed some policy autonomy in fiscal and public expenditure areas prior to 1972 under the old Unionist dominated Stormont parliament, under the new Agreement the northern power-sharing administration had very limited discretion over regional economic policy. Monetary policy in Northern Ireland and almost all elements of fiscal policy are set by UK norms, although there remained some discretion in the area of regional industrial and labour market policies, should the Executive wish to exercise them (The Agreement, 1998).

Strand 2

Strand 2 covers cross-border Irish/Northern Irish cooperation and the corner stone is the North–South Ministerial Council whose remit was described as follows:

To bring together those with executive responsibilities in Northern Ireland and the Republic of Ireland, to develop consultation, cooperation and action within the island of Ireland—including through implementation on an all-island and cross-border basis—on matters of mutual interest within the competence of the Administrations, north and south (Belfast Agreement, 1998).

This Council was designed to meet in different formats: in plenary format twice a year and in specific sectoral formats on a regular and frequent basis. The remit of the Council included the exchange of information, discussions and consultation on areas of cooperation;

the use of best endeavours to reach agreement on the adoption of common policies in areas where there is a mutual cross-border and all-island benefit; to take decisions by agreement on policies for implementation separately in each jurisdiction in relevant meaningful areas; and to take decisions by agreement on policies and action at an all-island and cross-border level to be implemented by other bodies to be established (Belfast Agreement, 1998).

During the transitional period between the first elections to the Northern Ireland Assembly in June 1998 and the full transfer of power to it in December 1999, it was intended that representatives of the Northern Ireland transitional administration and the Irish Government, operating in the North–South Ministerial Council, would undertake a work programme, in consultation with the British Government, with a view to identifying and agreeing on areas where cooperation and implementation for mutual benefit could take place. In an annex of Strand 2 in the Belfast Agreement, 12 possible areas where either new implementation bodies or the use of existing institutions and co-operative arrangements could be used are listed (Belfast Agreement, 1998). As part of its work programme, the Council was to identify and agree at least six matters for cooperation and implementation in each of the following categories:

(a) Matters where existing bodies would be the appropriate mechanisms for cooperation in each separate jurisdiction;
(b) Matters where the cooperation would take place through agreed implementation bodies on a cross-border or all-island level. The implementation bodies would have a clear operation remit and would implement on an all-island and cross-border basis policies agreed in the Council. (Belfast Agreement, 1998).

The Council was also to consider the EU dimension of relevant matters, including the implementation of EU policies and programmes and proposals under consideration in the EU framework. The views of the Council were also to be taken into account and represented appropriately at relevant EU meetings. Finally, the new Northern Ireland Assembly and the Irish Oireachtas (Parliament) were to consider developing a joint parliamentary forum and consideration was to be given to the establishment of an independent consultative forum appointed by the two Administrations, representative of civil society, comprising the social partners and others with expertise in social, cultural, economic and other issues.

The political sensitivities involved in drawing up the list of possible areas for North–South cooperation were clearly reflected from the start in the highly technical and tightly drawn nature of the suggested functions. In particular, the list seemed to reflect political compromises made between the opposing parties in the negotiations leading up to the Belfast Agreement (Coakley, 2002), rather than from a search for initiatives of potential strategic importance that might transform and dynamise North–South economic relations. This is seen most clearly, for example, by the absence of significant economic and industrial matters, in particular, issues such as the promotion of industrial development and the attraction of inward investment.[2]

Following intensive negotiations, an agreement was reached on 18 December 1998 on matters of North–South cooperation and cross-border policy implementation (Trimble & Mallon, 1998). The Trimble-Mallon statement of 18 December listed six North–South Implementation bodies: inland waterways, food safety, trade and business development, special EU programmes, language and aquaculture and marine matters. Finally, the Trimble-Mallon statement contained an initial list of six matters for North–South cooperation through the mechanism of existing bodies in each separate jurisdiction. These included non-controversial aspects of transport, agriculture, education, health, the environment and tourism.

A better understanding of the outcome of the Trimble-Mallon talks can be obtained from an earlier statement by the UUP First Minister, David Trimble, where he set out three principles that his party intended to apply to the selection and design of the cross-border implementation bodies (Trimble, 1998). First, any new body should have demonstrable advantages both for Northern Ireland and for the Republic of Ireland. Second, Northern Ireland's ability to develop a vibrant and competitive economy on a sound basis should not be impaired. Third, Northern Ireland's identity should not be submerged in a new all-Ireland identity.

The Belfast Agreement enshrined the principle that the people in Northern Ireland consented to the continued existence of Northern Ireland within the UK, and others, including nationalists, endorsed the legitimacy of that choice (Belfast Agreement, 1998).

While the logic of the first point—the necessity of mutual benefit—is obvious, the defensive logic of the second and third points—access to local policy instruments and regional identity—stands in contrast to the latest thinking on the dynamics of regional economic development where national and regional governments have a series of vital roles to play in promoting economic growth and development (Porter, 1998). So, the cross-border institutions set up under the Belfast Agreement, however beneficial, left many unresolved issues and appeared to have had only a weak impact on promoting desirable structural change and easing inter-community tensions.

East–West Cooperation and the Belfast Agreement: Strand 3

Strand 3 of the Belfast Agreement covered relations between Ireland and Great Britain, and took the form of a British–Irish Intergovernmental Conference, a British–Irish Council and an expanded British–Irish Interparliamentary Body (The Agreement, 1998, Strand 3, https://www.dfa.ie/media/dfa/alldfawebsitemedia/ourrolesandpolicies/northernireland/good-friday-agreement.pdf). Unlike the more formal institutions set up under Strands 1 and 2, these were consultative arrangements with no operational mandates or implementation mechanisms. Indeed, given the close economic and business relationships that already existed between Ireland and Britain, similar, if less formal, arrangements were already operating. The benefits to the Northern Nationalist community were that the Irish government could, under Strand 3, appear to be a political counterweight to the British government and, so to speak, be in their corner. However, the Strand 3 arrangements, albeit loose and with no real operational functions, stoked Unionist fear concerning their desire to be governed purely as a region of the UK.

Historical Economic and Political Background of the Belfast Agreement

The three main phases of post-independence strategic planning in Ireland never managed to exploit fully the opportunities of running a small, partitioned state that, for a very long time, was going to have to survive in the shadow of the hegemonic British power. So the Irish governments of 1922–1932 simply continued to run the economy of the Irish Free State in a *laissez faire* manner as an economic region of the UK (Fanning, 1996). The governments of 1932–1960 retreated behind high tariff barriers in an effort to accelerate local industrialisation by minimising links with the rest of the world. Ireland did industrialise during this period from an insignificant pre-independence base, but it never really modernised. After 1960, policy-makers were forced to address the failure of tariff protection as a means of robust and sustainable industrialisation (FitzGerald, 1968). Irish policy-makers encouraged foreign multinational firms to locate branch plants in Ireland, using low taxes on their profits and targeted assistance as the main incentives. The new policies were very successful, but they ignored and worked around the wider island development and infrastructural challenges created by partition and the dominant role of the British economy, rather than confronted it directly.

Close examination of the intellectual groundwork for Irish independence in 1922 (Kiberd & Matthews, 2016) reveals how little preparation was made by the revolutionaries for the *economic* governance of their wished-for state, as distinct from the goal of *political* detachment from British rule. With the exception of James Connolly, whose socialist programme had been articulated in detail in his extensive writings, the other leaders of thought and action during the pre-independence period were not much interested in business or economics (Connolly, 2008). Many in the independence leadership appeared to be blind to economic and business realities and indifferent to how they might be addressed in an independent state. Unfortunately, there was no equivalent of John Maynard Keynes to guide them, as Keynes had guided British policy-makers during the negotiation of the Treaty of Versailles and during WW-2 (Keynes, 2008; Skidelsky, 2000).

There were serious consequences of this neglect. In his *The Modernisation of Irish Society: 1848–1918*, Professor Joe Lee asks a damning question:

> Why did Ireland, outside the Lagan Valley, fail to create her own Bostons and Birminghams? Why did the population of Belfast increase from 100,000 to 400,000 between 1850 and 1914, while that of Dublin only managed to creep up from 250,000 to 300,000?

Professor Lee makes a compelling case for many internal societal failures rather than the more widely asserted external, British orchestrated restraints on Irish welfare and development (Lee, 2008). It is a telling measure of continuing failure that today we still live in the shadows of this nineteenth-century inability to map out acceptable economic and business options for the island of Ireland. The continuing dysfunctionality of the island economy today is partially a legacy of the enduring mistrust between north and south but also due to the absence of much by way of strategic analysis of the economic governance of the desired-for independent Ireland, combined with an inability or unwillingness to mitigate the consequences of the partition of the island. This shadow lay heavily over the formulation of the Belfast Agreement in the years before 1998 and today it still influences Northern Irish attitudes to Brexit.

Meanwhile, in Northern Ireland the economy faced a different, but no less serious set of challenges. After the phenomenal successes of the late nineteenth and early twentieth centuries in the north-east corner of the island, a long period of gradual de-industrialisation followed after WW-1, interrupted briefly by WW-2 but resumed thereafter (Bardon, 1992). There was a steady decline of the previous engineering, ship building, clothing and textiles success that had focused on Belfast and Derry and which had been a contributing factor in the process that drove partition. Civil unrest after 1968 accelerated the implosion of what remained of its early twentieth-century strong manufacturing base and an ever increasing subvention from London was needed to fill the gap created by the decline of the private sector by facilitating massive growth in public sector employment and consumer services.

Today, Ireland's external world has three key defining elements that are individually common to many small states, but taken all together are exceptional. First, its close relationship with the United States has facilitated the rise of a modern, export-oriented manufacturing and services sector, both through mainly US foreign direct investment and through spillovers into locally owned business enterprises. Second, the destinations for the exported products of these enterprises are predominantly within the European Union's Single Market (Bradley, 1996, p. 59). For example, much of North–South trade is in goods produced by indigenous Small Medium-Sized Enterprises (SMESs) that tend to focus on geographically close markets. Third, the relationships between Ireland and Northern Ireland have aspects that are specific to this island and differ from wider relationships between the regions of Britain and Ireland. For example, much of North–South trade is in goods produced by indigenous SMEs who tend to focus on geographically close markets. Northern Ireland's external world is similar, although the link to the US is weaker and NI–EU direct links are less developed. Links to Britain through external sales dominated, with Ireland being the largest foreign export destination (NISRA, 2017).

This was the economic context within which the Agreement talks were carried out. Policy-makers in Ireland were focused on the need to sustain growth and development within a small open economy in a rapidly evolving and integrating European Union.

Impact of the Agreement on Economic Development in Northern Ireland and Cross-border Cooperation

The decades following the Belfast Agreement were characterised by high optimism on the part of Northern policy-makers that the ravages of three decades of violence and destruction of much of the northern productive sector could be repaired quickly. There was much talk of a 'peace dividend' (O'Hearn, 2000). Investment would flow in. The underlying entrepreneurial culture of Northern Ireland would bounce back. And generous re-construction finance would be forthcoming from the UK treasury, from Europe and from America. Similarly, the Agreement's cross-border and East–West institutions were expected to foster increased economic cross-border cooperation. However, the argument made in this article is that the absence of general economic strategic planning in Northern Ireland has hindered both development and cooperation and that both are interlinked.

With an improved political situation in the north, the post-Agreement experience showed that the previous reluctance of individuals and groups to travel freely between both regions declined. Greatly increased North–South tourist flows, as Table 1 shows and the availability and increased traffic on the upgraded road and rail services were testimony to this process of North–South normalisation.

However, the impact of the Agreement on cross-border trade specifically was equivocal.

Table 1. Cross-border tourism: number of visitors in 000s 2000–2012

Year	North to South	South to North	Total
2000	465,000	189,000	654,000
01	513,000	199,000	712,000
02	557,000	205,000	762,000
03	586,000	224,000	810,000
04	569,000	252,000	821,000
05	613,000	271,000	884,000
06	626,000	277,000	903,000
07	638,000	322,000	960,000
08	636,000	367,000	1,003,000
09	985,000	475,000	1,460,000
10	1,189,000	454,000	1,643,000
11	1,304,000	370,000	1,674,000
12	1,264,000	430,000	1,694,000

Source: Inter Trade Ireland, http://www.intertradeireland.com/researchandpublications/trade-statistics/cross-border_tourism/.

Impact of Agreement on Cross-border Trade

Since the establishment of the North/South trade and business development body Inter Trade Ireland under the Agreement, some progress was being made in addressing the problem of market segmentation on the island. Trade literature in the south and the north was now targeted at disseminating information on marketing opportunities in both jurisdictions. Joint promotions of Irish products overseas were organised, and strategic alliances were encouraged between northern and southern firms. The distribution system on the island, which had in the past tended to deal with the north as part of the UK and with the south as a completely separate region, was gradually being integrated on an island-wide basis. In the longer term, the continued upgrading of strategic transport links on a partially co-ordinated all-island basis is likely to be another force for removing North–South market segmentation.

However, the potential gains in the future from greater North–South trade interaction, given existing northern and southern industrial specialisations, may be modest relative to the potential gains from greater penetration into wider world markets, including British markets. However, although the increase in trade from 2011 onwards is impressive and from 1995 to 2007, nevertheless, cross-border trade is small proportion of total trade for both economies, amounting to 5% approximately of total trade (Inter Trade Ireland, 2017). Table 2 shows levels of cross-border trade from 1996 to 2014.

The general statistics, however, mask the fact that cross-border trade is highly significant for certain sectors, such as agri-food and for local communities along the border. Moreover, North–South trading links have increased and deepened since the Belfast Agreement, and form an important, if under-appreciated element of both economies.

North–South trade improvement on the island is not an *alternative* to East–West trade improvement, but is entirely *complementary* to it. It is a transitional process that will produce gains in the short term and, by strengthening its supply side, will help to position the island economy to make further advances in world markets. North–South trade is likely to reach its potential if and only if the structure of manufacturing in both regions of the

Table 2. Total cross-border trade 1995 to 2014 (Inter Trade Ireland) (millions Euro)

1995	1345.7	1644.7
1996	1424.7	1758.64
1997	1536.9	2217.2
1998	1685.7	2487.9
1999	1740.9	2644.84
2000	1839.9	3021.53
2001	1852.1	2979.42
2002	1828	2908.2
2003	1874.1	2709.2
2004	2001.3	2949.76
2005	2089.8	3057.1
2006	2378.6	3489.47
2007	2598.9	3799.3
2008	2665.2	3355
2009	2378.7	2672
2010	2113.6	2465.27
2011	2224.6	2563.154
2012	2298.7	2834.7
2013	2436.2	2868
2014	2448.1	3071.8

Source: Intertrade Ireland, 2018, http://www.intertradeireland.com/researchandpublications/trade-statistics/total_cross_border_trade/.

island can evolve in a way that makes them more compatible and a source of increased inter-firm trade and not—as at present—trade in mainly consumer goods.

The Agreement and Economic Policy Making

It would be difficult to overstate the lack of progress in strategic socio-economic policy-making in Northern Ireland during the two decades after the signing of the Belfast Agreement. A policy document that captures the kind of internal development thinking during the first 10 years of the Agreement was *Strategy 2010*, a review of economic development policy in Northern Ireland that arose out of the Strand 1 of the Agreement (Department of Economic Development, 1999). Its remit was to encompass the entire economic context and set ambitious but attainable long-term goals for the Northern Ireland economy.

The report contained little new strategic thinking about the future relationship of the local economy with the external world, but a short section dealing with the UK economy contains a crucial assertion that coloured the thrust of the study:

The main determinant of economic activity in Northern Ireland is the level of activity in the rest of the UK. An economic development strategy for Northern Ireland therefore needs to be set within, and be consistent with, the overall thrust of national economic policy. (Department of Economic Development, 1999, p. 62)

This, in a nut-shell, was Northern Ireland's development dilemma. Either it stuck closely to UK economic policy and institutional norms, sometimes above, other times below UK average growth, or it struck out and sought a development strategy tailored to the very complex needs of the region.

After stripping away the rhetoric of partnership and consultation, *Strategy 2010* essentially came down to proposals for reformed or new institutions without providing analysis of how the old institutions were inadequate, together with a series of exhortations to the private sector to do better. The analysis upon which the report was based was at best partial, and at worst flawed. The diagnosis was unreliable and was not likely to form a basis for sound policy recommendations. The recommendations that were made lacked focus and involved no radical rethink about the policy framework that would be appropriate for a region like Northern Ireland, in the context of devolving governance within the UK and the growth and evolution of the economy of the island of Ireland (Bradley & Hamilton, 1999a, 1999b).

The early post-Agreement difficulties in designing an appropriate new development strategy for Northern Ireland have continued into the present. For example, the *Northern Ireland Economic Strategy* document that was published on 13 March 2012 by the then Minister of Enterprise, Trade and Investment, Arlene Foster, remains the current strategy and the fundamental blue-print for economic development policy in Northern Ireland for the immediate future (*Northern Ireland Economic Strategy*, 2012). Yet in it there are only two explicit references to the economy of Ireland: 'A large majority of sales outside NI are presently destined for either GB or the RoI, which is too narrow' (*Northern Ireland Economic Strategy*, 2012, p. 27) and 'Other countries such as Singapore and the Republic of Ireland (RoI) have developed their economies on the basis of a low corporation tax strategy and a pro-business regulatory environment' (*Northern Ireland Economic Strategy*, 2012, p. 31).

The 2014 Stormont House Agreement produced some progress (Stormont House Agreement, 2014) but, with one exception, the financial and economic policy measures agreed were mainly targeted at the internal political need to protect the population of Northern Ireland from the rigours of UK-wide fiscal retrenchment rather than on guiding the economy towards faster, sustainable, private-sector led growth. The exception was the proposal to permit Northern Ireland to impose its own rate of corporation tax, mainly to offset what is seen as the 'unfair' advantage of the low rate that applies in Ireland and its important role in attracting foreign direct investment.[3]

Knowledge that the future growth and success of the Northern Ireland economy will always be heavily dependent on its external trading links should not conceal the fact that these trading links are only likely to deliver prosperity and development if the internal economic governance of the region is focused, efficient and effective.

Worryingly, as a percentage of Northern Ireland Gross Value Added (GVA), the fiscal deficit in recent years is estimated to be in the region of 25–30% (Department of Finance Northern Ireland, 2017, http://www.dfpni.gov.uk/northern-ireland-net-fiscal-balance-report). This kind of regional deficit has persisted since the late 1970s and shows little sign of shrinking. Unlike the case of a sovereign state, where a public sector deficit of 30% of GDP would precipitate a major crisis of funding and would require immediate and drastic action, regional deficits of this magnitude can potentially continue indefinitely, so long as the nation-state, and the other surplus regions, in particular, were willing to fund it.

However, the Stormont House Agreement sets out a process that aims to reduce dependency and provides some tools that may revive export-oriented manufacturing and services, i.e. the option of having a lower rate of corporation tax in Northern Ireland. This would also have to include many other developmental measures in order to form a credible enterprise renewal strategy that would permit the economy of Northern Ireland to shift from dependency to self-sustaining autonomy.

The devolution of corporate tax rates contained in the Stormont House Agreement was intended to facilitate enterprise renewal in Northern Ireland. However, it was granted subject to two conditions: (i) The Northern Ireland block grant will be adjusted to reflect the corporation tax revenues foregone by the UK Government due to both direct and behavioural effects and (ii) The powers will only be granted, subject to the Executive demonstrating that its finances are on a sustainable footing for the long term including successfully implementing measures in this agreement and subsequent reform measures (Stormont House Agreement, 2014).

The first condition suggests that should Northern Ireland attract a large inflow of foreign or rest-of-UK investment, attributable to the lower rate of corporation tax, the block grant would be cut by an amount at least equal to total associated profits multiplied by the UK–NI corporate tax rate differential. The second condition makes tax devolution dependent on the successful implementation of UK-mandated budgetary austerity, and may cause political difficulties as the cuts are imposed on an economy still heavily dependent of public expenditure. Furthermore, if tax autonomy is given to other UK regions, the benefits to Northern Ireland would very likely be much attenuated.

There appears to be a deep reluctance on the part of some northern policy-makers to acknowledge the magnitude of the present systemic links across the border or to reflect on how these might be built up to generate further synergies for both jurisdictions. Such a narrow approach to growing the island economy may be politically driven within some circles of northern politics, but makes no sense from a business or economic perspective.

A measure of the failure of the economic side of the Agreement is that it produced a Northern Ireland economic strategy that continued to treat Ireland in much the same way as it treated Singapore. More specifically, attention is needed to address the peripheral state of the economy of the cross-border region, which is particularly disadvantaged by the historical legacy of the border. Far from being a minor issue, this is at the very core of the goal to renew the island economy in a mutually beneficial way. The reality is that both sides of the border region suffered after partition, while the rest of the island went its two separate ways. Until Irish and Northern Irish policy-makers bring themselves to address this historical legacy of distortion and disadvantage openly, honestly and effectively, cross-border bodies will continue to be symbolic and weak.

The Agreement has not brought about extensive economic cooperation, or development on the island economy. The argument in this article is that the root of this the failure lies not simply in Northern Irish politics and/or unionist objections to comprehensive and deep cooperation, but in the historical absence of a coherent and co-operative strategy in Northern Ireland and Ireland. In Ireland, there was a lack of any urgency to consider future island economic and business relationships, that stemmed from the foundation of the Irish state in 1922.

The Belfast Agreement, Cross-border Economic Cooperation and Brexit: An Uncertain Future?

Clearly, the Agreement's limited impact on economic development and cross-border cooperation has deep historical and public policy roots. In addition, to the challenges arising from these roots, there are numerous serious challenges arising from Brexit.

There are challenges for Northern Ireland in building on the economic and business links with Ireland, its second largest trading partner after Britain, at a time when its largest economic and trading partner—Britain—is likely to deviate increasingly from EU policy norms after it leaves the EU in 2019.

With respect to Irish/Northern Irish social and economic relations, the importance of Northern Ireland's trading and investment relations with Ireland mirror the similar importance of Ireland's trading and investment relations with the UK (including Northern Ireland). For example, small manufacturing and service firms on both sides of the border are able to trade in ways that would be more difficult if they were not geographically contiguous, relatively culturally homogeneous, and operating in an economic 'borderless' policy environment. Such firms are mostly indigenous (rather than foreign owned) and tend to be far more labour intensive than larger, internationally trading firms. Consequently, any disruption of such North–South links caused by changing UK–EU relations could have serious consequences (Bradley & Best, 2012).

In order to prepare for Brexit, some of the issues that urgently need to be put on the North–South institutional table include an integrated economic development strategy for the island that will reduce or even remove the policy fault lines that currently hinder industrial renewal in Northern Ireland, and address the excessive dependence on foreign direct investment in Ireland. However, the two relevant proposals contained in the Stormont House Agreement that relate to North–South and 'island' issues (i.e. the regeneration of the North–West region and the possible extension and reform of North–South bodies) are more in the nature of aspirations than concrete policy decisions and are unlikely to attract positive and enthusiastic cross-community support.

Conclusions on the Likely Future of the Agreement

One can envisage two extreme economic policy futures for Northern Ireland within the context of Brexit. The first would be 'more of the same': continued dependence, only marginal changes, agendas crowded by the mistrust, recrimination and divisiveness of history. The second would involve new and imaginative North–South synergies and would take place in a resurgence of this island that would make huge demands on both Northern Ireland and Ireland if it were to come about. It would be built on internal self-confidence and high trust. It would try to capture the synergies that the island economy undoubtedly has, but which history has never managed to capture.

The real fear is that the north with remain 'stuck in the middle' (to use Michael Porter's term from competitive strategy: Porter, 1998). Comfortable dependency may seem attractive to Northern Ireland in the short to medium-term, but has risks of a political and social kind that are likely to prevent the emergence of any will to change. But trying to break free in a way that creates a new dynamism in Northern Ireland may be seen as running even greater risks, even if it were politically feasible. It is more probable that efforts will be made to pursue both strategies simultaneously, with dependency dominating the emergence of any North–South synergies. History suggests this is unlikely to succeed and will leave both regions vulnerable to changes with which they are not prepared to deal.

Expectations were high in Northern Ireland after the implementation of the Belfast Agreement in 1998. There were hopes that the successful conclusion of the Agreement would provide the political institutions to bring about a new era of economic prosperity, perhaps re-capturing the dynamism and wealth of the period at the end of the nineteenth and start of the twentieth centuries, but this time for the whole island. However, the damage done to the economy of Northern Ireland during the 30 years of violence that broke out in 1968 and the legacy of political mistrust that it left in its wake appear to have been greatly underestimated at the time of the Agreement. As the drama and tension of the Agreement negotiations faded, the complex and challenging modalities of delivering change, openness and recovery became only too apparent, both to insider policy-makers as well as to outside observers. As regards future cross-border economic cooperation on the island of Ireland, the exact arrangements for the post-Brexit border have yet to be agreed between the UK government and the European Council. The very best that can be envisaged is broad maintenance of the *status quo ante*. But the more likely outcome is a deterioration of North–South economic cooperation and a disruption of East–West trading links between these islands, a scenario that the Agreement negotiators could scarcely have imagined.

Notes

1. A few days before the formal signing of the Agreement, the author received a call from one of the Irish government advisors to the negotiation team, enquiring if there were any business and economic cross-border topics that might be included.
2. It is interesting to note that the business community—north and south—argued that the *Belfast Agreement* did not go far enough in facilitating the economic and business initiatives that they had been promoting on a cross-border or island basis. Well before 1998, business people had already articulated the concept of a 'single island economy' (Quigley, 1992). At least in this context, the business community appeared to be ahead of politicians in seeing the logic of more extensive North–South economic cooperation.
3. The proposed new, low rate of corporation tax for Northern Ireland has not yet been implemented (November, 2017).

References

The Agreement. (1998). Retrieved from https://www.dfa.ie/media/dfa/alldfawebsitemedia/ourrolesandpolicies/northernireland/good-friday-agreement.pdf)

Bardon, J. (1992). *A history of Ulster*. Belfast: The Blackstaff Press.

Belfast Agreement. (1998). *Constitutional issues*. Retrieved from https://www.dfa.ie/media/dfa/alldfawebsitemedia/ourrolesandpolicies/northernireland/good-friday-agreement.pdf

Bradley, J. (1996). *An island economy: Exploring long-term consequences of peace and reconciliation in the island of Ireland*. Dublin: Forum for Peace and Reconciliation.

Bradley, J., & Best, M. (2012, March). Cross border economic renewal: Rethinking Irish regional policy. Centre for Cross Border Studies, p. 284. Retrieved from http://www.crossborder.ie/pubs/2012-economic-report.pdf

Bradley, J., & Hamilton, D. (1999a). Strategy 2010: Planning economic development in Northern Ireland. *Regional Studies, 33*(9), 885–890.

Bradley, J., & Hamilton, D. (1999b). Making policy in Northern Ireland. *Administration, 47*(2), 32–50.

Coakley, J. (2002). *The North-South institutions: From blueprint to reality. Working paper no. 22*. Dublin: Institute for British-Irish Studies, University College Dublin.

Connolly, J. (2008). *Socialism and the Irish Rebellion: Writings from James Connolly*. St Petersburg, FL: Red and Black Publishers.

Department of Economic Development. (1999). *Strategy 2010: Report by the economic development strategy review steering group on Northern Ireland*. Belfast: Author.

Department of Finance Northern Ireland. (2017). Retrieved from http://www.dfpni.gov.uk/northern-ireland-net-fiscal-balance-report

Fanning, R. (1996). *The Irish Department of Finance*. Dublin: Institute of Public Administration.

FitzGerald, G. (1968). *Planning in Ireland*. Dublin: Institute of Public Administration and London, Political and Economic Planning.

Inter Trade Ireland. (2017). Retrieved from http://www.intertradeireland.com/researchandpublications/trade-statistics/cross-border_tourism/

Intertrade Ireland. (2018). Retrieved from http://www.intertradeireland.com/researchandpublications/trade-statistics/total_cross_border_trade/

Keynes, J. M. (2008). *The economic consequences of the peace*. London: BiblioLife.

Kiberd, D., & Matthews, P. J. (2016). *Handbook of the Irish revival: An anthology of Irish cultural and political writings 1891–1922*. Notre Dame, IN: University of Notre Dame Press.

Lee, J. (2008). *The modernisation of Irish society 1848–1918: From the great famine to Independent Ireland*. Dublin: Gill Books.

Northern Ireland Economic Strategy. (2012). *Priorities for sustainable growth and prosperity*. Belfast: Stormont.

Northern Ireland Statistics and Research Agency. (2017). Broad economy sales and export statistics. Belfast. Retrieved from https://www.nisra.gov.uk/publications/current-publication-broad-economy-sales-exports-statistics

O'Hearn, D. (2000). Peace dividend, foreign investment and economic regeneration: The Northern Irish case. *Social Problems, 47*(2), 180–200.

Porter, M. (1998). *On competition*. Boston, MA: Harvard Business Review Press.

Quigley, W. G. H. (1992, February 28). Ireland—an Island Economy. Paper presented at the Annual Conference of the Confederation of Irish Industry, Dublin.

Skidelsky, R. (2000). *John Maynard Keynes: Fighting for Britain 1937–1946*. London: Macmillan.

Stormont House Agreement. (2014). Dublin: Department of Foreign Affairs and Trade. Retrieved from https://www.dfa.ie/media/dfa/alldfawebsitemedia/ourrolesandpolicies/northernireland/20151223-Stormont-House-Agreement—Document.pdf

Tannam, E. (1999). *Cross-border cooperation in Northern Ireland and the republic of Ireland*. Basingstoke: Palgrave.

Trimble, D. (1998, November 19). *Speech by the First Minister*. Dublin: Chamber of Commerce of Ireland.

Trimble, D., & Mallon, S. (1998, December 19). Statement issued by the First Minister and Deputy First Minister towards implementing the Belfast Agreement, as published in the *Irish Times*, Saturday.

The EU's Influence on the Peace Process and Agreement in Northern Ireland in Light of Brexit

KATY HAYWARD & MARY C. MURPHY

ABSTRACT   The UK's withdrawal from the European Union (EU) has enormous implications for Northern Ireland. All sides to the Brexit negotiations quickly agreed that it was vitally important to protect the peace process and to uphold the 1998 Good Friday (Belfast) Agreement. However, the question of how this was to be done soon became a point over which there were very apparent differences between the two sides; such differences are manifest within Northern Ireland in differing political views regarding European integration and national sovereignty. This paper explores the effects of EU membership on the peace process and the Agreement in light of the Brexit process. It provides an overview of the difficulties and frictions in finding a common approach from Northern Ireland to the EU and explains how this is manifest in the response to the Brexit referendum of June 2016. It concludes by considering some of the ways in which the Agreement itself offers means of navigating some of the more thorny issues arising as a result of the UK's withdrawal from the EU.

Introduction

The 1998 Good Friday (Belfast) Agreement has had far more significance than making the Irish border less visible—it has redefined relations across these islands in a way that has defused the border as a cause for political conflict and violence. Crucial to this was the context provided by the UK and Ireland's membership of the European Union (EU). For common membership of the EU meant that both states were, essentially, heading in the same direction, especially in areas that relate to cross-border movement.

On 4 September 2017, the Irish Minister for Foreign Affairs, Simon Coveney, and Michel Barnier, the Chief Brexit Negotiator for the EU, held a joint press conference in Brussels. At it, Barnier made efforts to emphasise the significance of the outcome of the Brexit negotiations to the peace process in Northern Ireland. He stated:

Our aim is to ensure that the Common Travel Area and Good Friday Agreement (of which the UK has a special responsibility as co-guarantor) are not affected by the UK's decision to leave the Union.[1]

As there was a lack of progress in the Brexit negotiations, so the EU's rhetoric regarding the protection of Northern Ireland/Ireland appeared to grow in forcefulness and determination. In the same press conference, Barnier's description of 'Ireland's concerns' as 'the Union's concerns' effectively positioned the EU as a defender and guarantor of the Agreement, even as it was conducting negotiations with the UK.

The process of making the EU a protector of the Agreement is a fascinating one—and one that was surely not envisioned when the referendum on the UK's withdrawal from the EU was first posited. As many commentators have pointed out, the EU plays, at best, a bit part in the text of the Agreement. It was not a contributor to the negotiations behind the Agreement, nor was EU membership given particular significance in the outworking of its tenets. That said, the fact that relations across Britain and Ireland have become so much closer and more intertwined as a result of common membership of the EU means that the ambition of ensuring the Agreement will be 'unaffected' by Brexit is only realisable if there is a very narrow interpretation of the Agreement itself. Indeed, it was by design that both British and Irish states formally expressed their joint commitment to the 1998 Agreement as 'friendly neighbours and as partners in the European Union'.[2] Common membership of the EU meant that both states, essentially, shared a common vision for their respective futures, and this meant agreement on objectives and actions across a wide array of public policy. Both states were effectively bound together by a shared future within the EU; thus cross-border cooperation enabled Irish and British nationalisms to be entangled without either one being eroded. In light of this broad and complex context, this paper assesses the implications of Brexit for the Agreement, and the relevance of the Agreement for Brexit. It begins by summarising the importance of the EU for Northern Ireland and the peace process itself.

The EU and Northern Ireland

Historical Roots of Tentative Engagement

Northern Ireland was experiencing profound political instability during the early years of UK and Irish accession to the EU in 1973. Membership coincided with the introduction of direct rule from Westminster in Northern Ireland and the intensification of violence. As a consequence, the prospects of membership were only minimally discussed and considered. The early years of being part of the then European Economic Community (EEC) were marked by similarly low levels of interest and engagement. In the Stormont debating chambers, there was some discussion of matters European prior to UK accession, but these were invariably coloured by domestic political considerations or 'channelled into traditional arguments' (Hainsworth, 1983, p. 56). The Social Democratic and Labour Party (SDLP) was the only Northern Ireland political party to engage positively with the prospects of EEC membership from an early stage (see McLoughlin, 2009), partly on the grounds that it offered the chance to place the conflict on the international stage. In contrast, the then-dominant Ulster Unionist Party (UUP) largely ignored the new European context, making only scant reference to the EEC in their 1973 election manifesto (Murphy, 2009, p. 594). This indifference was also apparent beyond party politics. Guelke (1988, p. 155) has concluded that 'there was a relatively muted reaction in the province to actual entry to the Community'. Instead, political positions on Europe were filtered through long-held views on sovereignty and national identity.

1998–2018: Northern Ireland's Limited Engagement with the EU

Despite the significance of the EU for the peace process, ideological divides on the constitutional status of Northern Ireland hindered deeper engagement with the EU.

The pattern of viewing European integration through the prism of nation-state focused discourses has persisted throughout EU membership. Indeed, the Brexit referendum debate encapsulated this, with the gradual polarisation of unionist and nationalist positions on the matter (Gormley-Heenan & Aughey, 2017). More generally, the predominance of nationalist/unionist ideological positions in discourse on European integration has meant that the nuances and detail of EU membership have tended to be overlooked, under-considered and even downplayed in Northern Ireland. Added to this, the legacy of the conflict and fractious community relations have shaped the engagement of the political classes with the subject of EU membership. It is therefore understandable as to why the very topic of Brexit—let alone the *process* of withdrawal—is highly problematic as well as contentious in post-Agreement Northern Ireland.

Public knowledge of the EU in Northern Ireland and attitudes towards membership have also tended to reflect those of the largely disinterested political classes. A 2003 survey revealed that only one-tenth of respondents professed to have an interest in the EU; of these, the largest proportion had such interest purely on the grounds of EU finances/grants/funding (McGowan & O'Connor, 2004, p. 34). The tone and content of media coverage of the EU is also a factor in shaping public attitudes. Murphy (2014, p. 189) notes that when it comes to the transmission of EU information in Northern Ireland: 'An information deficit exists and this is exacerbated by press and media coverage which often reinforces misinformation.' The Eurosceptic stance of much of the British tabloid media is a factor in that it has infiltrated the Northern Ireland market, contributing to an often skewed public conversation. The overall quality of EU discussion and dialogue in Northern Ireland, therefore, lacked substance and reliability.

Perhaps exacerbated by this lack of information, the persistent fact is that attitudes towards European integration have traditionally followed the communal divide in Northern Ireland—unionists have always been more Eurosceptic than nationalists (although Sinn Féin's position has vacillated, in line with leftist critiques and the traditional nationalist argument that sovereignty is eroded by EU membership) (see Hayward & Murphy, 2010). In the past, this difference of opinion has not tended to be problematic because it did not demand deeper consideration of complex political questions related to UK sovereignty, the unity of the UK, and constitutional issues. This has all changed with the topic and process of the UK's withdrawal from the EU.

Significance of the EU for the Peace Process

British–Irish Intergovernmental Cooperation and EU Membership

Even as the EU had a low profile in Northern Ireland and was seen by the majority as irrelevant to the conflict, it acted as a unique catalyst for bilateral discussions between the UK and Irish governments. The European Parliament (EP) produced an interesting analysis of the Northern Ireland conflict in its Haagerup Report (1984), emphasising the importance of both British and Irish dimensions in the conflict and in any quest for resolution (Hayward, 2006). Accordingly, following the signing of the Anglo-Irish Agreement in 1985, the EU pledged both economic and political support to the process.

As Tannam notes (2018), the practice and the EU provided a model of intergovernmental relations in the EU that helped strengthen British–Irish relations to the benefit of peace in Northern Ireland. Notwithstanding public disagreements, British–Irish relations moved towards a shared acceptance of a consensual approach to matters of common concern and shared EU membership was important for this. The 1985 Anglo-Irish Agreement itself noted the 'determination of both governments to develop close cooperation as partners in the European Community'. Nowadays it is entirely normal and expected that Irish ministers and officials will play a major role in negotiations and talks on the peace and future of Northern Ireland. The fact that common EU membership has been crucial in securing the legitimacy and respect for an input from the Irish state into the peace process has new relevance in light of Brexit.

Related to this, perhaps the most crucial influence the EU has had on the resolution of the conflict in Northern Ireland has been 'constructive' but indirect, affecting the structures, context and language of conflict resolution among regional level actors (Hayward, 2007; Hayward & Diez, 2008). This reflects the nature of the EU as a diverse organisation whose substantial effects are determined at the level of the recipient. It also reflects the nature of the conflict in Northern Ireland itself, which required a peace process that works at various levels in order to achieve common interests through political cooperation. Ultimately, it appears that it is not so much the actors or structures of the EU but *the actual process of European integration itself* that has served to facilitate cooperation across ideological, political and territorial borders.

The Material Impact of the EU on the Peace Process

In addition to changing the environment and means for British–Irish cooperation, the EU has been successful in forging change in cross-border economic relationships in Ireland in very practical ways. This has most clearly come through its structural impact on the significance of the border as an economic and customs divide. For example, the introduction of EEC regulations on customs declarations in 1987 had an immediate effect on the ease with which goods could be transported between north and south. Furthermore, the creation of the Single Market on 1 January 1993 erased many obstacles to cross-border trade and economic development. Added to this, the EU helped create, support and fund networks and programmes across and through the border region, helping to ameliorate some of the negative legacies of the border while facilitating closer integration of economies on either side.

From the late 1980s, Northern Ireland became a beneficiary of new opportunities for EU financial assistance. Northern Ireland was long regarded as a priority region for EU structural fund assistance (see Trimble, 1990). The 1988 reform of the structural funds confirmed this by classifying the region as an 'Objective 1' region, a title it retained until 1999. In an unusual move, the EU reacted to the paramilitary ceasefires of 1994 by committing the 'carrot' of additional targeted financial aid to the region. The PEACE programme was created in 1995 and linked economic support to peace-building. As such, the PEACE programmes can be regarded as 'specifically designed conflict transformation tool[s]' (Buchanan, 2008, p. 387). They have financed a range of measures including economic regeneration, social inclusion and cross-community cooperation, and they are rooted in local and regional partnership arrangements. The Special EU Programmes Body (SEUPB) was a cross-border implementation body created under the terms of the 1998 Agreement to oversee this work.

More broadly, across the Irish border and the Irish Sea, freedom of movement of labour, goods, services and capital have been dramatically expanded; these have been grounded in the legal realities of EU membership and manifest in the processes of regulatory harmonisation, standardisation and mutual recognition that affect business on the ground. Added to this, EU investment in border regions and cross-border programmes benefitted the Irish border region in tangible ways. This is why EU membership has meant so much more for the peace process than simply its economic support, or the removal of customs posts along the border. That said, the EU has rarely been credited for the course of the peace process. This is in no small part due to the fact that the Northern Ireland political classes and administration have held the EU at arm's length. And the 1998 Agreement did not alter this situation significantly.

The introduction of devolution in 1999 changed Northern Ireland's constitutional status within the UK. The region was granted advanced decentralised powers managed by a directly elected cross-community Assembly and Executive. This move demanded much of Northern Ireland's political parties and personnel. It required the new administration to engage more robustly with a 'normal' policy agenda, and less with constitutional and security issues. For the first time in generations, Northern Ireland politicians began to grapple with a range of pressing socio-economic challenges across policy portfolios including health, education, welfare, the environment, and more. The governance arrangements which pertained until the signing of the 1998 Belfast Agreement did not facilitate a high degree of regional autonomy vis-à-vis the EU. Nonetheless, the newly created institutions and the revised structure of administrative units required some engagement with the EU dimension to Northern Ireland public policy responsibilities. This was slow to materialise and initially focused heavily on establishing a Northern Ireland presence in Brussels.

The Office of the Northern Ireland Executive (ONIEB) opened in Brussels in the early 2000s. This was supported by the work of what was then the European Policy Coordination Unit (EPCU) in the Executive Office and the Northern Ireland Assembly's Committee of the Centre which in 2002 conducted a European Inquiry and produced a Report. The latter included important prescriptions for the development of a Northern Ireland–EU strategy. Murphy (2007, p. 311) notes that during this period there were 'subtle degrees of institutional adaptation, the gradual evolution of formal and informal linkages and changes to the process of policy making and decision making'. Importantly, these developments were elite led—awareness and engagement did not typically extend beyond political and administrative elites.

The Northern Ireland–EU relationship entered a new era following the re-establishment of devolved institutions in 2007, after a protracted five-year period of suspension. The period is marked by two contradictory themes—dynamism and discord (see Murphy, 2018). The dynamism is evident in terms of increased engagement between the Northern Ireland administration and the EU authorities in Brussels. Another significant dynamic was in the development of constructive relations between the ONIEB and the Irish Permanent Representation (Perm Rep) in Brussels (Murphy, 2011, p. 562). The ability of the Northern Ireland Executive to draw on two Permanent Representatives for at least informal support exemplifies the unique position of Northern Ireland, and the immense goodwill it enjoyed even a decade after the Agreement.

The re-establishment of the devolved institutions in 2007 prompted the European Commission to create the Northern Ireland-EU Taskforce (NITF). The NITF created a strategic partnership between Northern Ireland and the Brussels based institution. The initiative was an express attempt, on the part of the Commission, to support and help consolidate the return to devolved power in Northern Ireland (Hayward & Murphy, 2012). By strategically connecting Northern Ireland interests and Commission officials, the NITF facilitates improved engagement with the EU by prompting agreement on a series of Northern Ireland–EU actions, strategies and forward-planning exercises. During this period too, the scope of Northern Ireland's external relations has expanded, particularly with respect to the Republic of Ireland. On EU issues, there now exist a culture of information sharing, regular political contact, and the emergence of shared all-island positions between the two jurisdictions. However, although there is a more proactive approach to the EU in Northern Ireland, there are also limits. Input by Northern Ireland political parties to the UK government's policy in advance of the Brexit referendum, and following it, was highly limited, and this was despite the significance of a UK withdrawal from the EU for the Irish border and Northern Ireland.

Limited Action and Capacity

Beyond utilitarian motivations to avail of EU funding, the Northern Ireland administration has often been characterised by inaction on some key EU issues and initiatives. This has in part been a consequence of an incapacity to recognise opportunities/threats from outside the UK context and, secondly, as a result of home-grown political disputes and disagreements between the two largest political parties, the Democratic Unionist Party (DUP) and Sinn Féin. This sporadic inability to agree common actions and approaches to EU matters has constantly hindered Northern Ireland from feeding effectively into wider UK–EU discussion and debates. The UK government's decision to overlook the Northern Ireland issue during and after the EU referendum exacerbated the situation.

This lack of Northern Ireland input is notably evident in the *Balance of Competences Review* (2014) which examined the balance of competences between the UK and the EU. The UK government review was an analytical exercise which investigated how the EU affects British life in 32 areas, from health and education to the economy. The government's laudable aim in this review (of deepening public and parliamentary understanding of the nature of the UK–EU relationship and contributing constructively and seriously to the national debate concerning possible reform of the EU) was manifestly not met. Even where parts of the review do form a more robust component of the wider debate around UK–EU membership, a Northern Ireland voice is hardly present. This is because the contribution of the Northern Ireland administration to the *Balance of Competence Review* was at best limited, at worst non-existent. For example, the Northern Ireland Executive did not contribute to the 'Subsidiarity and Proportionality' consultation exercise, despite its clear relevance and applicability to the devolved region.[3] Where submissions had been made, they tended to be short, narrow in their analysis and guided by Northern Ireland economic concerns. Their tone was also largely pro-EU (even when delivered by a DUP Minister), favouring either a continuation of the status quo or refinement of existing practices.

Clear support for withdrawal from the EU was certainly not in evidence from Northern Ireland at the time.

The contents of the review may have informed Prime Minister David Cameron's attempts to renegotiate the terms of UK–EU membership in 2015. The extent to which the devolved administrations contributed to or influenced the national UK negotiating position is unclear. Avenues for regional input have existed for some time, most notable among these are intergovernmental structures, especially the Joint Ministerial Committee on Europe JMC[E]. This connects the centre of UK government with the devolved regions and has included means by which Welsh, Scottish, and Northern Ireland devolved administrations contribute to discussions on EU matters. The weight and import of these discussions in deciding the national position are less easy to trace. What is clear is that in the past, the forum has not always operated satisfactorily. For instance, the then Prime Minister was heavily criticised in 2012 for failing to use established links to discuss the UK approach to the Fiscal Treaty negotiations. More recently, Prime Minister Theresa May was criticised for failing to advise the devolved administrations of her intention to trigger Article 50 in March 2017.

The 2016 EU Referendum in Northern Ireland

The Context, the Campaign and the Fallout

The decision by the former UK Prime Minister David Cameron to hold a referendum on UK membership of the EU in 2016 kick-started a debate on the merits and otherwise of the UK's relationship with the EU. It was an ill-tempered and divisive referendum campaign. Slow to develop and lacking in energy and dynamism, the Northern Ireland referendum campaign produced only a low level of public debate and largely failed to engage the general public. The situation was further antagonised by the position of the Northern Ireland Secretary of State, Theresa Villiers, who opposed the Remain position adopted by the Prime Minister and supported Brexit. This also exposed a division on the island between north and south, where the British government's representative in Northern Ireland was at variance with the majority of parties in Northern Ireland and with the position being pursued by the Irish state, which had been proactive in pushing for the UK to remain in the EU. Overall, the 2016 UK referendum on EU membership highlighted divisions between the Northern Ireland parties and the low priority of Northern Ireland for the UK government's campaign and the British electorate.

Even with a suitable forum for constructive input from the Northern Ireland administration, and even with implicit agreement among the parties that the UK should remain in the EU, a clear Northern Ireland position on vital EU matters was never forthcoming due to the lack of internal agreement. Unlike Scotland or Wales, *the cross-party nature of the Northern Ireland Executive has severely limited the articulation of a single Northern Ireland position*. For example in 2014, even before the Prime Minister conducted negotiations with the EU prior to the Brexit referendum, the Scottish government (2014) strongly endorsed continued UK membership of the EU and published *Scotland's Agenda for EU Reform* by way of input to the broader UK debate. In contrast, the Northern Ireland administration did not articulate a position on the negotiations or the referendum question. Across a host of EU-related policy issues, from the single currency to migration to social Europe, the parties to the Northern Ireland Executive were left to express differing views and perspectives. Sporadic internal political crises further undermined any prospects for even minimal cross-party consensus on the EU question.

These difficulties are further evident in the Northern Ireland Assembly. The 2014/2015 strategic priorities of the Committee of the Office of First Minister and Deputy First Minister (OFMDFM) did not reference the EU, even in the shadow of the impending Brexit referendum. The Northern Ireland Assembly also hosted the biannual meeting of the European Committee Chairs UK forum where topics of mutual interest including EU reform and the referendum on EU membership were discussed. The Northern Ireland Assembly Enterprise Committee (2015) did commission research on the economic implications for Northern Ireland of a Brexit. The Briefing Note (produced by the Open University) estimated that economic output in Northern Ireland would be 3% lower in the event of a UK departure from the EU. However, no Assembly inquiry was initiated and no opportunities for widespread consultation and debate were taken up. Instead, this task was assumed by the Northern Ireland Affairs Committee of the House of Commons, which launched a wide-ranging inquiry into the issues affecting Northern Ireland in the context of the Brexit referendum. Its report concluded (2016, p. 86):

> The peace process has ultimately been successful because of the commitment of successive UK and Irish governments and the willingness of politicians and the communities they represent to put aside past differences sufficiently to allow Northern Ireland to be governed peacefully.

Unfortunately, setting aside differences in order to articulate the interests of Northern Ireland itself proved to be an extremely difficult 'ask' in the shadow of Brexit.

The referendum campaign in Northern Ireland focused predominantly on the implications of Brexit for the border between Northern Ireland and the Republic of Ireland, free movement of people and trade, and the impact of a UK exit on the fragile peace process. The question of EU funding, particularly future access to structural funds, the PEACE Programme and the Common Agricultural Policy, also featured in campaign debates (McCann & Hainsworth, 2017). The issue of immigration—which so animated the campaign across England—was not a key talking point in Northern Ireland. Overall, the EU referendum campaign in Northern Ireland was very much grounded in voters' traditional political and constitutional allegiances (Carmichael, 2016, p. 87):

> Ultimately, therefore, the majority of the electorate in Northern Ireland behaved largely by reference to the issue which defines politics here, namely, the constitutional question and the border with the Republic of Ireland.

The Referendum Result

From the early days, there was an expectation that the Vote Remain camp would win the plebiscite, and probably do so decisively. The referendum result, however, delivered an unexpected outcome. By a slim margin of 51.9%, the UK voted to leave the EU. In contrast to the UK as whole, however, Northern Ireland returned a 55.8% majority vote to remain.

The Northern Ireland result was in fact lower than had been anticipated by pollsters, and so too was the turnout figure. At 62.7%, the Northern Ireland turnout rate was almost 10 percentage points lower than for the UK as a whole. The breakdown of the result demonstrates, however, that the profile of voters who supported Remain was similar for other parts of the UK. Those who supported the UK staying in the EU tended to be younger, better educated and in better-paid jobs. In terms of party political preferences, Northern Ireland voters appear to have heeded the cues from local political parties. DUP voters were strongly in favour of Leave while nationalist voters were strongly in favour of Remain. All constituencies represented by a nationalist or independent MP returned a vote in favour of continued EU membership. The UUP, unlike the larger DUP, advised voters to vote in favour of continued EU membership but not all UUP supporters heeded this advice. The seven constituencies which voted Leave were those with Unionist majorities and represented by Unionist MPs.

The EU referendum result in Northern Ireland is interesting because although political persuasion was broadly an indicator of voter choice, it did not produce evidence of a stark communal divide on the question of continued EU membership. Research by Mills and Colvin (2016) and Garry (2017) notes that possibly one-third of Unionists chose Remain which suggests that in terms of political preference, there existed some shared perspective between unionist and nationalists. In the aftermath of the referendum outcome, however, nationalists, and Sinn Féin in particular, railed against the decision, demanding that the will of the Northern Ireland electorate be respected. In contrast, Unionists, including the UUP that had campaigned for Remain, accepted the result as the sovereign decision of the entire UK. We thus saw the cementing of polarisation in political discourse towards the EU that had always been present in Northern Ireland.

The Referendum Fallout

Overall, Northern Ireland was wholly unprepared for the challenges of Brexit. In particular, the ability of the Northern Ireland administration to respond swiftly and constructively to a potentially serious economic threat has been limited. The Northern Ireland Executive failed to produce a comprehensive assessment of the impact of Brexit on Northern Ireland, and the administration was also unable to agree a clear Northern Ireland negotiating position. Acknowledgement of Brexit is also absent in terms of future regional economic planning, for example, Economy 2030 (2017), the Industrial Strategy for Northern Ireland consultation document, contains little or no assessment of the risks associated with Brexit. The most significant contribution from the Northern Ireland Executive to the Brexit process took the form of a two-page letter from the First and deputy First Ministers (Arlene Foster and Martin McGuinness) to the Prime Minister in August 2016. In it they stated their:

> wish to play a part in the engagement between the two Governments on the unique aspects of the negotiations that arise from the border, recognising the possibility that it cannot be guaranteed that outcomes that suit our common interests are ultimately deliverable. We wish to have full access to that intergovernmental process as the border issues affecting trade, employment, energy and potential criminality are of such high significance for us.[4]

Unfortunately, the collapse of the Executive in early 2017, the subsequent hindrance of the North South Ministerial Council, the limited role of the Joint Ministerial Committee on EU negotiations, and the caution regarding British–Irish contact through the process of the EU negotiations made such objectives quite unrealisable from an early stage. Moreover, the common ground found for this letter quickly evaporated as the Brexit debate in the UK as a whole became increasingly characterised by patriotic rhetoric rather than constructive detail—an environment that would only ever add toxicity to political discourse within Northern Ireland.

The lack of common ground among the political parties in Northern Ireland on Brexit was only worsened by the collapse of the Executive in the wake of the scandal around the Renewable Heating Initiative. The results of the subsequent Assembly election on 2 March 2017 saw two major changes to the makeup of the Northern Ireland Assembly: unionist parties no longer in the majority in Stormont and MLAs from Remain parties out-number those from pro-Leave parties with a margin that better reflects the 56% Remain outcome in the Brexit referendum. However, the predominant effect of Brexit has been to deepen antagonism between the parties, not least because of the grassroots differences between their supporters (around 85% of Catholic/Irish/Nationalist voters supported Remain compared to 38% of Protestant/British/Unionist voters) (Garry, 2017).

These divisions were further exacerbated by the snap General Election in June 2017, which saw the eradication of the SDLP and UUP from representation in Westminster, meaning that the only seats taken up by Northern Ireland MPs in the House of Commons were from the DUP (alongside the independent MP Lady Sylvia Hermon). The confidence and supply deal between the DUP and Conservative Party required to give the governing party a Commons majority commits the DUP to supporting any emer-ging agreement with the EU. The most immediate effect of this deal was to see very close links between the DUP and the Tory party, especially in a strong pro-Brexit approach, and the subsequent weakening of trust from nationalists in Northern Ireland regarding the potential outcome of the Brexit process. The failure to restore the Executive was particu-larly serious in the light of Brexit's potential implications for the Agreement.

The Agreement and Brexit

The impact of Brexit is such that two states will now diverge, leaving Northern Ireland in the awkward place between. After Brexit, without a careful arrangement for managing UK/EU (and British–Irish) relations, divergence will happen in law, trade, security, values, the fundamental rights of citizens, and politics—all such areas reach to the very core of the Good Friday Agreement and put it at risk of deep fissures.

Within months of the Brexit referendum, a legal case was made (led by Raymond McCord) regarding the implications of Brexit for the terms of the 1998 Agreement.[5] It argued that readjusting or revising the Agreement (and the attendant Northern Ireland Act of 1998) in order to purge references to EU law and policy (specifically for North–South relations on the island) could potentially unravel what is arguably an ambiguous and tactical toleration between political protagonists. The case was unsuccessful because the matter was seen as not a legal problem in and of itself, and the need for consent for changes to the constitutional status of Northern Ireland as only having effect in relation to its relationship to the Republic of Ireland (not the EU).

Yet, a narrow legal interpretation of the role of the EU in the Agreement does not prop-erly represent the full significance of the EU for the post-Agreement social, political and institutional environment of Northern Ireland. The EU is quite so important for the Agree-ment because it created the context within which such cross-border cooperation was normalised and depoliticised. The fact that nationalists felt themselves equal and protected as Irish citizens in Northern Ireland has been in no small part connected to the broader framework of common EU citizenship. At its most general, the division present in nationalist and unionist interpretations of EU membership is reflected in their diverging approaches to Brexit—a divergence that has only become more pronounced as the negotiations continued. A year after the Brexit referendum result, there was even less common ground between (pro-Leave) unionists and (pro-Remain) nationalists than before it. It was in the use of the EU as a point of deepening divergence between the two communities that the risk posed to the Agreement by Brexit was most direct and most acute.

Official Positions on the Agreement and Brexit

In recognition of the dangers of Brexit for the Agreement—and in response to the proactive efforts of the Irish Government to raise the profile of the matter of the Irish border and Northern Ireland in Brussels—the matter of Northern Ireland/Ireland was made one of the three top priorities for the first phase of the Brexit negotiations (alongside citizens' rights and financial liabilities). The European Council elaborated on this in its Guidelines for the Brexit negotiations (2017, p. 11):

> The Union has consistently supported the goal of peace and reconciliation enshrined in the Good Friday Agreement in all its parts, and continuing to support and protect the achievements, benefits and commitments of the Peace Process will remain of paramount importance.

The EP has done likewise, expressing concern for the consequences of Brexit on Northern Ireland and relations with Ireland, and stating that: it is crucial to safeguard peace and therefore to preserve the Good Friday Agreement 'in all its parts'.[6]

The UK Government's White Paper on leaving the EU published in February 2017 (see HM Government, 2017a), and a position paper on Northern Ireland/Ireland in the negotiations issued in August 2017 (see Hm Government, 2017b), were criticised by the EU for being limited in scope and depth and presenting little in the way of a definitive strategy. The government's position paper on Northern Ireland/Ireland stated (paragraph 10):

> The UK believes that the UK Government, the Irish Government and the EU share a strong desire to continue to safeguard the Belfast ('Good Friday') Agreement, and to ensure that nothing agreed as part of the UK's exit in any way undermines the Agreement.

Using the type of 'constructive ambiguity' that the 1998 Good Friday (Belfast) Agreement is famed for, the UK Government's Position Paper on Northern Ireland and Ireland does acknowledge the need for some form of bespoke arrangements for Northern Ireland after Brexit. Furthermore, it openly engages with the EU's language of finding 'flexible and imaginative solutions', even if only with direct reference to avoiding a 'hard border'.

On the preservation of the Agreement, the emphasis seemed to be on the right of Irish citizens in Northern Ireland to continue to enjoy full rights as European citizens. In the absence of agreement with the EU on the rights of citizens after Brexit, and of any detail on the Common Travel Area arrangements for Irish citizens in the UK, such reassurances had little clout. More broadly, the British government's core principles: the preservation of the peace process; no return to the borders of the past; seamless and frictionless borders, were rehearsed and repeated in various statements, position papers and speeches, but there remained a lack of clarity as to how these principles can find expression in the final UK–EU 'divorce settlement'. The Irish government also managed to have agreement from both the EU Council and from the UK government that the possibility of Irish reunification (secured in the 1998 Agreement) will not be undermined by Brexit and that Northern Ireland would become part of the EU if this occurred. Such agreements point to the uniqueness of Northern Ireland but they also serve to further stimulate expressions of opposing political opinion regarding the constitutional future of Northern Ireland. The joint report agreed between the UK government and EU negotiators in December 2017, which facilitated movement to the second phase of withdrawal negotiations, has been the most concrete statement of support for the Good Friday Agreement.[7] It explicitly notes the broad importance of the Agreement and states (paragraph 50):

> The United Kingdom will ensure that no new regulatory barriers develop between Northern Ireland and the rest of the United Kingdom, unless, consistent with the 1998 Agreement, the Northern Ireland Executive and Assembly agree that distinct arrangements are appropriate for Northern Ireland.

This acknowledges a pivotal role for the institutions created by the Agreement and affords them centrality in terms of agreeing future arrangements for dealing with Brexit challenges unique to Northern Ireland.

The Agreement as a Foundation for Solutions

Taking a lesson from the Agreement itself, constructive ambiguity may be a way of facilitating some sort of creative agreement between the two parties where neither side is seen to either win or lose, and where key unionist and nationalist principles can be maintained according to their own interpretation. In this way, achieving and implementing an agreement in relation to some form of specific arrangements for Northern Ireland may be possible. For all parties to agree, any such arrangements would have to differ from the proposals put forward by Sinn Féin and the SDLP for Northern Ireland holding special status within the EU after the UK's withdrawal. Nonetheless, the political parties in Northern Ireland share some common perspectives regarding the most favourable outcomes from Brexit. The OFMDFM letter of August 2016 reflects the fact that all parties in Northern Ireland want to avoid a hard border, want to see the free movement of people, want to safeguard the agri-business sector, and want to protect the integrated electricity market. Where nationalists favour special status for Northern Ireland, unionists (including those who voted Leave) wish to see continued cooperation with the Republic of Ireland based on: 'common aims such as a seamless, frictionless border and maintenance of the common travel area' (DUP, 2017, p. 4). There is some potential overlap between these two positions.

More broadly, there is a great deal in the Agreement that creates the conditions for flexible and imaginative solutions, including those relating to citizenship, rights, equality of opportunity. Indeed, 20 years on, several promises of the Agreement remain unrealised: a Northern Ireland Civic Forum, a north/south Consultative Forum, and the possibility of bilateral or multilateral arrangements between members of the British–Irish Council. Some argue that such initiatives—already agreed in principle—offered the means of safely navigating the changes made by Brexit across these islands (Hayward & Phinnemore, 2017). The Joint Oireachtas Committee on the Implementation of the Good Friday Agreement (2017) also touched on these issues in its report examining the impact of Brexit and called for 'renewed impetus' in relation to the continued implementation of aspects of the Agreement.

The Agreement explicitly recognises that the political aspirations and identities and rights of Irish and British residents in Northern Ireland are formally recognised as equal and with parity. This is an important point of relevance for the Brexit discussions: the opinions and preferences of one grouping should not trounce those of the other. The question then comes into play: how best to preserve the equality of Irish people in Northern Ireland after Brexit? This is not just about citizenship; there are many more in Northern Ireland who claim an Irish identity than who hold Irish passports. Moreover, those born in Northern Ireland have a birth-right to be Irish. The territory of Northern Ireland has a unique standing in that regard—one that looks directly threatened by growing divergence between Britain and Ireland. How can it be protected? By considering it as a meeting point between the two. Facilitating this 'British–Irish meeting point' would mean nurturing the Agreement's institutions, and in particular preserving and enhancing the capacity of the British–Irish and North/South bodies. This would allow the institutions to develop into vital places for communication, strategy-creation, and policy coordination between the various constituencies. Crucially, this would represent a strengthening, rather than an undermining of Northern Ireland's novel power-sharing arrangements. It would cement existing cross-border and cross-national relationships so essential to the peace process.[8] To some extent, the joint report agreed between the UK government and EU negotiators offers the potential for this type of dynamic to emerge. The document states: 'The people of Northern Ireland who are Irish citizens will continue to enjoy rights as EU citizens, including where they reside in Northern Ireland' (p. 52). Suggestions of a role for the institutions of the Good Friday Agreement in shaping aspects of the Brexit process which pertain to Northern Ireland's unique circumstances also offers an opportunity for strengthening and enhancing key facets of the Agreement, even as Northern Ireland is extracted from the context of EU membership.

Conclusion

Within the context of European integration, Irish/Northern Ireland cross-border cooperation was depoliticised and normalised. Outside of this context, such cooperation is not only more difficult in practical terms, it becomes symbolically and politically more sensitive. Indeed, because cross-border cooperation will then require political will and action at several levels on both sides of the border, it can both be (a) less likely to happen and (b) subject to misinterpretation or over-egging by political opponents and political friends. This carries particular risks in a divided society such as Northern Ireland, where political capital still rests on emphasising adherence to a particular view of the Irish border. Drawing attention to the border—and making it subject to politicking in this way—is something that only critics of the peace process are keen to do. The Agreement itself has been sustained by British and Irish involvement in its implementation, and by the incentives offered by joint EU membership. Brexit challenges and potentially undermines key tenets of that settlement. The EU will no longer provide a context for dialogue, cooperation, and support. Consensus must be built to navigate the uncertainty and the changes entailed in the process of Brexit.

This will no doubt require the type of flexibility and compromise that have had to be found in earlier periods of crisis in Northern Ireland. While the short-term temptation is to seek a recourse to unionist/nationalist ideology and rhetoric, the long-term consequences of the decision that are taken now could not be greater for post-Agreement Northern Ireland. The joint UK–EU report agreed in December 2017, which sets the stage for stage two of the withdrawal negotiations, provides a tentative framework within which consensus not just within Northern Ireland might be agreed, but also between the Northern Ireland administration and the UK, and between the UK and the EU. Twenty years on from the Agreement, Northern Ireland faces its most challenging test to date—and one that comes, quite unexpectedly, from political machinations outside Northern Ireland.

Funding

This work was supported by the Economic and Social Research Council [ES/P009441/1] 'Between two unions: The Constitutional Future of the Islands after Brexit'.

Notes

1. 'Barnier and Coveney hold press conference in Brussels (04/09/2017)', *Mikk Media News Network*. Retrieved October 18, 2017, from https://www.youtube.com/watch?v=fZq_HIDTeXg.
2. This explicit reference to the European Union is contained in the 'Agreement between the Government of the United Kingdom of Great Britain and Northern Ireland and the Government of Ireland' which forms part of the Good Friday Agreement, signed 10 April 1998. Retrieved October 20, 2017, from https://www.dfa.ie/media/dfa/alldfawebsitemedia/ourrolesandpolicies/northernireland/good-friday-agreement.pdf.
3. The Scottish government, Welsh government and National Assembly of Wales all submitted evidence to the consultation. In its contribution, the Scottish government noted:

   We consider that the Call for Evidence issued by the Foreign & Commonwealth Office in respect of subsidiarity and proportionality is one of the most important aspects of any review of the balance of competences between the EU and its Member States

   Retrieved December 8, 2017, from https://www.gov.uk/government/consultations/subsidiarity-and-proportionality-review-of-the-balance-of-competences.
4. The letter is available on the website of the Northern Ireland Executive. Retrieved October 19, 2017, from https://www.executiveoffice-ni.gov.uk/publications/letter-prime-minister-rt-hon-theresa-may-mp.
5. The details of the two applications for judicial review are available here: https://www.courtsni.gov.uk/en-GB/Judicial%20Decisions/PublishedByYear/Documents/2016/%5B2016%5D%20NIQB%2085/j_j_MAG10076Final.htm.
6. This reference is contained in Paragraph E of the EP resolution of 3 October 2017 on the state of play of negotiations with the United Kingdom (2017/2847(RSP)). Retrieved December 8, 2017, from http://www.europarl.europa.eu/sides/getDoc.do?pubRef=-//EP//TEXT+TA+P8-TA-2017-0361+0+DOC+XML+V0//EN&language=EN.
7. The joint report was published on December 8, 2017. Retrieved December 8, 2017, from https://ec.europa.eu/commission/sites/beta-political/files/joint_report.pdf.
8. For comparison, this has worked well for the Nordic Council, which has some members who are in and others who are out of a range of different supranational blocs such as NATO, the EU, and the EEA.

References

Anglo-Irish Agreement. (1985, November 15). Retrieved from https://www.dfa.ie/media/dfa/alldfawebsitemedia/ourrolesandpolicies/northernireland/Anglo-Irish-Agreement-1985-1.pdf

Buchanan, S. (2008). Transforming conflict in Northern Ireland and the border counties: Some lessons from the peace programmes on valuing participative democracy. *Irish Political Studies*, *23*, 387–409.

Carmichael, P. (2016). Reflections from Northern Ireland on the result of the UK referendum on EU membership. In M. Guderjan (Ed.), *The future of the UK: Between internal and external divisions* (pp. 82–101). Berlin: Humboldt University.

Department for the Economy (Northern Ireland). (2017). *Economy 2030: A consultation on an industrial strategy for Northern Ireland*. Belfast: Author. Retrieved from https://www.economy-ni.gov.uk/sites/default/files/consultations/economy/industrial-strategy-ni-consultation-document.pdf

DUP. (2017). *Our plan for Northern Ireland: The DUP manifesto for the 2017 Northern Ireland assembly election*. Belfast: Author.

European Council. (2017, April 29). *European Council (Art. 50) guidelines for Brexit negotiations*. Retrieved from http://www.consilium.europa.eu/en/press/press-releases/2017/04/29/euco-brexit-guidelines/#

Garry, J. (2017). *The EU referendum vote in Northern Ireland: Implications for our understanding of citizens' political views and behaviour*. Northern Ireland Assembly Knowledge Exchange Seminar Series, 2016–2017. Retrieved from http://www.niassembly.gov.uk/globalassets/documents/raise/knowledge_exchange/briefing_papers/series6/garry121016.pdf

Gormley-Heenan, C., & Aughey, A. (2017). Northern Ireland and Brexit: Three effects on 'the border in the mind'. *The British Journal of Politics and International Relations*, *19*, 497–511.

Guelke, A. (1988). *Northern Ireland: The international perspective*. Dublin: Gill and Macmillan.

Hainsworth, P. (1983). Direct rule in Northern Ireland: The European Community dimension 1972–79. *Administration*, *31*, 53–69.

Hayward, K. (2006). Reiterating national identities: The European Union conception of conflict resolution in Northern Ireland. *Cooperation and Conflict*, *41*, 261–284.

Hayward, K. (2007). Mediating the European ideal: Cross-border programmes and conflict resolution on the island of Ireland. *JCMS: Journal of Common Market Studies*, *45*, 675–693.

Hayward, K., & Diez, T. (2008). Reconfiguring spaces of conflict: Northern Ireland and the impact of European integration. *Space and Polity*, *12*, 47–62.

Hayward, K., & Murphy, M. C. (Eds.). (2010). *The Europeanization of party politics in Ireland, north and south*. London: Routledge.

Hayward, K., & Murphy, M. C. (2012). The (soft) power of commitment: The EU and conflict resolution in Northern Ireland. *Ethnopolitics*, *11*, 439–452.

Hayward, K., & Phinnemore, D. (2017). *Brexit necessitates an Agreement-plus for Northern Ireland*. UK in a Changing Europe. Retrieved from http://ukandeu.ac.uk/brexit-necessitates-an-agreement-plus-for-northern-ireland/

HM Government. (2014). *Balance of competences review*. Retrieved from https://www.gov.uk/guidance/review-of-the-balance-of-competences

HM Government. (2017a). *The United Kingdom's exit from and new partnership with the European Union*, Cm 9417. Retrieved from https://www.gov.uk/government/uploads/system/uploads/attachment_data/file/589191/The_United_Kingdoms_exit_from_and_partnership_with_the_EU_Web.pdf

HM Government. (2017b, August 16). *Northern Ireland and Ireland: Position paper*. Retrieved from https://www.gov.uk/government/publications/northern-ireland-and-ireland-a-position-paper

House of Commons Northern Ireland Affairs Committee. (2016, May 26). *Northern Ireland and the EU referendum*. First Report of Session 2016–2017, HC 46. Retrieved from https://publications.parliament.uk/pa/cm201617/cmselect/cmniaf/48/48.pdf

Joint Oireachtas Committee on the Implementation of the Good Friday Agreement. (2017). *The implications of Brexit for the Good Friday Agreement: Key findings, 32/JCIGFA/01*. Retrieved from http://data.oireachtas.ie/ie/oireachtas/committee/dail/32/joint_committee_on_the_implementation_of_the_good_friday_agreement/reports/2017/2017-06-22_the-implications-of-brexit-for-the-good-friday-agreement-key-findings_en.pdf

McCann, G., & Hainsworth, P. (2017). Brexit and Northern Ireland: The 2016 referendum on the United Kingdom's membership of the European Union. *Irish Political Studies*, *32*, 327–342.

McGowan, L., & O'Connor, S. (2004). Exploring Eurovisions: Awareness and knowledge of the European Union in Northern Ireland. *Irish Political Studies*, *19*, 21–42.

McLoughlin, P. (2009). The SDLP and the Europeanization of the Northern Ireland problem. *Irish Political Studies*, *24*, 603–619.

Mills, E., & Colvin, C. (2016, 18 July). *Why did Northern Ireland vote to Remain?* QPol. Retrieved from http://qpol.qub.ac.uk/northern-ireland-vote-remain/

Murphy, M. C. (2007). Europeanisation and the sub-national level: Changing patterns of governance in Northern Ireland. *Regional and Federal Studies, 17,* 293–315.

Murphy, M. C. (2009). Pragmatic politics: The Ulster Unionist Party and the European Union. *Irish Political Studies, 24,* 589–602.

Murphy, M. C. (2011). Regional representation in Brussels and multi-level governance: Evidence from Northern Ireland. *The British Journal of Politics and International Relations, 13,* 551–566.

Murphy, M. C. (2014). *Northern Ireland and the European Union: The dynamics of a changing relationship.* Manchester: Manchester University Press.

Murphy, M. C. (2018). *Europe and Northern Ireland's future; negotiating Brexit's unique case.* London: Agenda.

Northern Ireland Assembly Enterprise Committee and the Open University. (2015). *The Consequences for the Northern Ireland economy from a United Kingdom exit from the European Union.* Briefing Note, CETI/OU, 2/15 March. Retrieved from http://crossborder.ie/site2015/wp-content/uploads/2015/11/2015-03-22-brexit-ceti-specialist-advisor.pdf

Scottish Government. (2014). *Scotland's Agenda for EU Reform.* Retrieved from http://www.gov.scot/Resource/0045/00458063.pdf

Tannam, E. (2018). Intergovernmental and cross-border civil service cooperation: The Good Friday Agreement and Brexit. *Ethnopolitics.* doi:10.1080/17449057.2018.1472422

Trimble, M. (1990). The impact of the European Community. In R. Harris, C. Jefferson, & J. Spencer (Eds.), *The Northern Ireland economy: A comparative study in the economic development of a peripheral region* (pp. 416–439). London: Longman.

Brexit, Bordering and Bodies on the Island of Ireland

CATHAL MCCALL

ABSTRACT   The Brexit campaign to withdraw the United Kingdom from the European Union (EU) was driven primarily by opposition to immigration and the freedom of movement of EU workers to Britain. Consequently, a central focus of Brexit was the perceived need for bordering, that is, the strengthening of Britain's borders as security barriers to prevent the movement of these unwanted outsiders to Britain. Such bordering has the potential to turn the tide against decades of debordering on the island of Ireland that was delivered by Europeanisation, the North South provisions of the Good Friday Agreement and a wealth of cross-border cooperation initiatives. From an open Irish border vantage point, this paper explores three Brexit bordering options: bordering the United Kingdom of Great Britain and Northern Ireland; bordering Britain and bordering the isles of Britain and Ireland. The argument is that the least costly one is to confine Brexit bordering to the island of Great Britain.

Introduction

Traditionally, modern state territorial borders have been understood as parameters of possession, protection and exclusion in the national imagination. Within these borders, the national group inhabits the territory, seeks to preserve it from incursion by unwanted outsiders and sanctifies it as 'ours, not theirs' through its collective memories and associated emotions (Berezin, 2003, p. 7). Freedom of movement of labour across European Union (EU) borders captured a substantial segment of the British national imagination because it is held responsible for breaching the imagined parameters that give meaning to Britain, Britishness/Englishness and the contemporary 'British way of life'.

This paper examines Brexit bordering options to control the movement of bodies with human faces. It does so from the vantage point of an Irish border that has been the subject of Europeanisation, the North South provisions of the Good Friday Agreement and a wealth of cross-border cooperation initiatives for two decades, resulting in a border that has been reconfigured from control barrier to connecting bridge.

Debordering: Europeanisation, the Good Friday Agreement and Cross-Border Cooperation

Fundamentally, Europeanisation encapsulates the creation, empowerment and influence of intergovernmental and supranational EU institutions. Europeanisation stresses concerted economic, legal, political and cultural action above the state, and intergovernmental cooperation between member states. It also encompasses cross-border cooperation between border regions, cities and localities. All have important implications for the meaning of sovereignty and the complexion of modern state borders within the EU (Keating, 2004; Sørensen, 1999; Wallace, 1999).

According to Vladimir Kolossov, borders configured as barriers are 'not only inefficient but objectively harmful to society and the economy' (Kolossov, 2005, p. 619). The 1986 Single European Act was pivotal in reconfiguring member state borders from 'hard' tariff and security barriers to 'soft', open, free-flowing economic bridges. This reconfiguration was required in order to facilitate the flow of goods and people, and thus operationalise a European 'Single Market' (O'Dowd, 2002, p. 20). After the introduction of the European Single Market on 31 December 1992, border customs posts were abandoned, marking a visible and significant reconfiguration of member states' borders from 'hard' to 'soft'.

From 1989, the EU's structural funds initiative Interreg has promoted regional, city and local level cross-border cooperation in an effort to help address and erode 'from below' administrative, political, cultural and emotional obstacles to the creation of a Single Market (Phinnemore & McGowan, 2013, p. 304). On the island of Ireland, the EU Peace Programmes (from 1995) boosted such cooperation for the purpose of peacebuilding after conflict. These cross-border cooperation initiatives further progressed Irish border reconfiguration from barrier to bridge through their promotion of mobility, contact, communication and cooperation across it. The Peace programmes alone have provided funding of €1,524 million over almost two decades with cross-border cooperation prioritised. Two decades of hard and soft capital cross-border bridge-building has given substance to the notion of cross-border cooperation as conflict amelioration and helped to underpin the Good Friday Agreement's peacebuilding credentials (McCall, 2011)

The Agreement itself provided an infrastructural framework for cross-border cooperation on the island of Ireland. The North South (island of Ireland) structure was a key provision of the Agreement. It comprises of the North South Ministerial Council and its Implementation Bodies. Meetings of the North/South Ministerial Council have been concerned with North South cooperation in education, health, transport, agriculture, the environment and tourism, and have involved ministers with sectoral responsibility for each. Meanwhile, the Implementation Bodies promote North South cooperation in the areas of trade and business development, food safety, Gaelic and Ulster-Scots languages, aquaculture, waterways and EU Programmes.[1] A limited company—Tourism Ireland—functions as a de facto implementation body to promote the island abroad as a tourist destination (Coakley, Ó Caoindealbháin, & Wilson, 2007; Laffan & Payne, 2001).

While the Agreement nominally reaffirmed UK sovereignty over Northern Ireland in the formal-legal sense, the North South institutions were clearly aimed at spreading the political and cultural substance of sovereignty beyond the state (Ruane & Todd, 2001, p. 936). Thus, debordering the Irish border has involved constitutional ingenuity, reimagining state sovereignty and overcoming borders as barriers to mobility, contact, communication, cooperation and trade. It was bolstered by the eventual removal of the selective border security regime in the early 2000s.

The launch of the European Single Market in 1992 and the onset of the Irish Peace Process in 1994 meant that border customs posts and border security checkpoint instillations were surplus to requirements. Secondary roads were re-opened and militarised sections of the Irish border gradually became demilitarised through the dismantling of British Army mountain top watchtowers in South Armagh and the closure of heavily fortified security bases along the border (Nash, Reid, & Graham, 2013, pp. 109–111). The result is that the physical manifestation of the Irish border itself is hardly discernible save for a change in road markings and some 'Welcome to Northern Ireland' signs erected by the Northern Ireland Department of Regional Development in 2012, though many of these signs were removed, vandalised, defaced or, in one instance, riddled with bulletholes.[2]

The continuing insurgent activity of small Irish republican splinter groups in the border region thereafter did little to disrupt the transformation of the Irish border from barrier to bridge. For example, in August 2009, one such group left a 300 kg bomb outside Forkhill, County Armagh, running a concealed command wire across the border into County Louth. A telephone warning was given but a week passed before British security forces located the bomb. Upon the discovery, the UK Government asserted that British troops would not be reintroduced to secure the Irish border.[3]

Since the Good Friday Agreement, police cooperation across the Irish border has thrived through informal networks and force-to-force agreements, though largely without overarching transparent regulatory and accountability structures and processes. Primarily, its focus has been on organised crime and the activities of continuing republican insurgents. One example of this cooperation is the cross-border investigation into the murder of Paul Quinn by a criminal gang south of the border in 2007. An Garda Siochána (Irish Police) and Police Service of Northern Ireland (PSNI) officers operated as a team with Gardai conducting door-to-door enquiries in Northern Ireland (accompanied by PSNI personnel) while PSNI officers attended the interviews of suspects and witnesses in Ireland (Walsh, 2011). Another example of organic cross-border cooperation involving police officers was the prolonged search in 2016 for the body of a young man believed to have drowned in the river Erne which traverses the Irish border. Police and burgeoning numbers of people from both sides of the border joined forces in the search which ended after two months when the body was found. In the intervening period, strong bonds of friendship were forged with one police officer commenting 'we saw these people realising that there is very little actually separating us' (Pollak, 2016).

From the perspective of bodies with human faces, the benefits of debordering the Irish border cannot be over-estimated. The day-to-day cross-border mobility, contact, communication and cooperation among people has been beneficial to society, not least through its significance in supporting the Irish Peace Process, especially when unionist–nationalist political disagreements impacted upon the functioning of the Good Friday Agreement institutions (McCall, 2011).

Rebordering: Brexit

On the broader European and global fronts, the EU's debordering impulse of the 1990s was challenged by twenty-first-century dramatisations that gave rise to increased perception of risks and threats from international terrorism and contested immigration. The EU response was to attempt to create the EU as a 'gated community'. It deploys sophisticated selection mechanisms which determine the entry of individuals, the aim being to protect European citizens from multifarious threats emanating from beyond the gates (van Houtum & Pijpers, 2007, p. 303). In the process, cross-border cooperation may be understood to have shifted from being a debordering dynamic towards a bordering one through the increased emphasis on border securitisation across the EU's external frontier (Andreas, 2003; McCall, 2014; Walters, 2006). Thus, while the EU has 'sought to valorize transnational spaces through cross-border and inter-regional co-operation programmes' (Keating, 2010, p. 30), its twenty-first century emphasis on 'security' has translated into building an EU external frontier as a barrier against multifarious threats.

Borders remain the principal foci for securitising mobility (Amoore, 2006). Indeed, many EU member states have attempted to take border matters into their own hands and secure their state borders in the face of contested immigration and terrorist attack. These attempts have been understood as performances in reasserting the authority of the state (Peoples & Williams, 2015, p. 175). They confirm that debordering and rebordering are competing and overlapping processes in the EU (Amilhat Szary & Giraut, 2015, p. 4).

The campaign for the UK to leave the EU—commonly referred to by the acronym 'Brexit' (from 'Britain's exit')—was invigorated by concerns, prejudices, fears and insecurities relating to the mobility of EU workers, as well as a media spotlight on contested immigration, in the contexts of a prolonged period of economic austerity and the EU's Mediterranean migration/refugee crisis which spiked in 2015.

The Brexit referendum campaign focused on the nexus between bordering and security. Its primary objective was to establish a hard security border regime in order to prevent the movement of unwanted outsiders to Britain, including those coming from within the EU, and thus remove an 'existential threat' to British identity (Buzan, 1993).

The Brexit referendum on 23 June 2016 resulted in a majority of 52 per cent in favour of the UK exiting the EU. Michael Keating detected three groups under the Brexit umbrella: the 'Europeans' who prioritise access to the European single market without the political consequences[4]; the 'Little Englanders' who oppose EU membership or affiliation; and the 'Globalists' who resent EU regulation and believe that the UK can become a global economic superpower in its own right (Keating, 2016). However, objection to the EU's freedom of movement of labour principle was a key motivating factor for Brexiters of all hues.

The threat from contested immigration has made regular headlines in the British media, particularly in the right-wing tabloid press. Calais, Sangatte and 'the Jungle' have been portrayed as sites of perennial threat for Britain and 'the British way of life'.[5] Chaotic scenes of contested migrants attempting mass crossings of the English Channel via the Channel Tunnel have provided the necessary drama for prioritising this issue in British politics. Reacting to this drama in July 2015, the then UK Prime Minister David Cameron heightened it further when he proclaimed that ' ... you have got *a swarm* of people coming across the Mediterranean, seeking a better life, wanting to come to Britain because Britain has got jobs, it's got a growing economy, it's an incredible place to live' (my emphasis).[6] Such a 'speech act' has been identified as an important component of a securitisation process that emphasises bordering (Waever, 1995): 'the swarm' is the threat; hard security borders are the answer to that threat.

The wider issue of the post-2004 arrival of 'legitimate' mobile workers from Central Eastern Europe is the prejudicial bedrock upon which this securitisation process is based.

According to Cameron: ' ... the bigger issue today is migration from within the EU. Numbers that have increased faster than we in this country wanted ... at a level that was too much for our communities, for our labour markets'.[7]

According to Roger Liddle, the Brexit campaign was 'the remorseless logic of Conservative division on the European question' (Liddle, 2015, p. 5). It was a direct consequence of the strength of Eurosceptic lobbies within the Party and beyond it. With Cameron leading a Conservative majority government after May 2015, Brexit became firmly placed on the UK political agenda with the EU freedom of movement of labour principle becoming an important motivating factor of the campaign (O'Ceallaigh & Gillespie, 2015, p. 223).

In the UK, the state security bordering process was already well advanced, symbolised by large signs declaring 'The UK Border' in the international arrivals halls of UK airports. The UK border security regime is a sophisticated response to perceived threats emanating from *Outre-Mer* and is largely focused on 'border portals' and 'choke points'—airports, ports and the Channel Tunnel. The Channel Tunnel is a particular point of interest for those concerned with bordering Britain to halt contested immigration. Unlike a land border, the Channel Tunnel is a singular port of entry or 'choke point' through which all vehicles, goods and people have to pass and, as such, should present a relatively straight-forward site for the exercise of a security regime (Anderson with Bort, 2001, p. 184). A greater challenge is patrolling the maritime borders around Britain, especially when it was revealed that the Border Force fleet numbered only five sea-worthy vessels.[8]

The British border security regime also involves activities in an electronic/intelligence cyberborder sphere, with nodes that extend to the European continent, and wherein the biometric passport—'the border in the pocket'—and the smartphone with GPS supersede many traditional functions of the human border guard (Häkli, 2015, p. 93).

Yet, Brexiters remained unimpressed by 'the border in the pocket' or by the fact that the UK border zone extends territorially to the European continent with UK border guards, replete with a formidable armoury of electronic border control paraphernalia—information databases, X-ray machines, electronic fingerprinters, body scanners, heat-seeking cameras, robots and probes—stationed in Boulogne, Brussels, Calais, Coquelles, Dunkerque, Frethun, Lille and Paris. They are blind to the work of border intelligence agents, such as Airline Liaison Officers who advise foreign law enforcement agencies on the potential cross-border movement of people deemed to be 'illegitimate' or 'undesirable' travellers (Vaughan-Williams, 2009). And it is, of course, a top priority of British Intelligence agencies, engaged in the clandestine governance of border control, to remain below the radar of politicians, the media and the general public.

Conversely, Brexiters have enjoyed a high profile in British politics and the media; their cause helped by the Mediterranean migration/refugee crisis, by arresting television images of contested migrants attempting to cross the English Channel and by the *Polski Smak* (Polish Flavour) of the rapidly changing twenty-first-century British high street. In other words, efforts to create an eclectic border zone around Britain through offshore bordering practices did not neutralise the perceived threat posed by legitimate mobile EU workers to the contemporary 'British way of life'.

The 'bring back control' quest of Brexiters demands the creation of clear, hard security borders that prove to be impenetrable for unwanted outsiders, including those from within the EU. But where would the Brexit security border run?

Option 1: Bordering the United Kingdom of Great Britain and Northern Ireland

Britain's front door to the European continent is heavily alarmed and would readily serve many of the bordering requirements of Brexit. Britain being an island lends itself to bordering. However, the UK's back door to Ireland is wide open. The barely perceptible Irish border is the only land border that the UK shares with another member state.[9]

Prior to the Brexit referendum, then British Home Secretary Theresa May claimed that 'it is inconceivable that a vote for Brexit would not have a negative impact on the North/South [Irish] Border, bringing cost and disruption to trade and to people's lives'.[10] After becoming Prime Minister, May acknowledged that ' ... of course Northern Ireland will have a border with the Republic of Ireland, which will remain a member of the European Union'.[11]

Post-Brexit, Ireland will continue as an EU member state and abide by its freedom of movement obligations. So it is, therefore, logical to assume that the Irish border will be the principal foci for the British Government's effort to 'bring back control'. However, this assumption is problematic, not least because the Irish border meanders for approximately 500 km through towns, townlands, mountains, loughs, bogs, fields, farms and houses across the island of Ireland, has hundreds of crossing points, and was the subject of agitation and violence from its consolidation in 1925 until its reconfiguration from barrier to bridge in the 1990s. The island of Ireland has the densest cross-border road network in Europe (Leary, 2016). Additionally, it is unruly: key arterial roads can cross the border more than once. For example, the direct route from Cavan Town (in Ireland) to Dungannon (in Northern Ireland), through the Drummully Salient, crosses the border no less than 5 times.

When the Northern Ireland 'Troubles' shifted from urban centres to the Irish border region in the 1980s British security forces had difficulty coping with local mobile Irish Republican Army units whose members had an in-depth knowledge of the complex border terrain (Patterson, 2013). Additionally, the border security regime was partial because the British Government recognised that a continuous securitised border would play into the hands of Irish republican insurgents since it would have risked further alienating the Irish nationalist population. In other words, the relative lack of border security was due to the fact that there was 'no political will at Westminster' for its imposition because of the concern that such a move would further stir political and militant Irish nationalism (Rose, 1983, p. 3).

With 'no political will at Westminster' to secure the Irish border at the height of the Northern Ireland 'Troubles', such an undertaking after Brexit would be a demonstration of abject political neglect. All the more so because the reconfiguration of the Irish border from barrier to bridge—through the removal of security checkpoints and customs posts, as well as the Good Friday Agreement's promotion of North South (Belfast–Dublin) and cross-border cooperation—has been an important element in British–Irish peacebuilding.

Conceivably, Brexit bordering could entail the reintroduction of customs, agri-food inspection and immigration checkpoints on cross-border arterial routes, the closure of hundreds of secondary cross-border roads (that were re-opened in the 1990s courtesy of EU Interreg funding),[12] and the establishment of a border security regime to support vulnerable customs and inspection officials and infrastructure.

Technology could be applied to the management of Irish border security. Devices such as motion sensors, scanners, infra-red and surveillance cameras, as well as migration databases could be deployed in that management. Indeed, the Legatum Institute—the influential

Brexit 'think tank' in London—proposed the 'persistent surveillance of the border region' by Unmanned Aerial Vehicles (drones) after Brexit[13] (Singham, Morgan, Hewson, & Brooks, 2017, p. 28). However, to suggest that technology would render a post-Brexit Irish border 'invisible' is rejected by border technology experts (Taylor, 2017). Without the human border guard, sensors, scanners, cameras and databases serve as little more than recording and counting devices of border crossings (Broeders, 2011, pp. 40–41). Additionally, in the case of the unwieldy Irish border, technological infrastructure on cross-border roads would be no less vulnerable to destruction than 'Welcome to Northern Ireland' signs unless it was protected by human border patrols.

In its EU–UK Brexit negotiations Position Paper *Northern Ireland and Ireland* (2017), the British Government stated that it wanted the Irish border to remain 'as seamless and frictionless as possible'. If this statement reflected a desire to maintain the *status quo*, namely, an open border with the free flow of goods and people across it, then there is an obvious clash with the British Government's greater desire: leaving the EU (including the Single Market and Customs Union) and 'taking back control' of the free movement of people. Since Brexit has been inspired by the desire to curb freedom of movement of labour from the European continent it does not seem plausible that the UK Government could entertain the continuation of an open Irish border. Nigel Lawson, the former UK Chancellor of the Exchequer and chairman of the Vote Leave campaign, conceded that 'there would have to be border controls'. Dominic Raab, Parliamentary Under Secretary of State at the Ministry of Justice between May 2015 and July 2016, also admitted that 'If you're worried about border controls and security … you couldn't leave a back door without some kind, either of checks there with any country or assurances in relation to the checks that they're conducting, obviously'.[14]

Option 2: Bordering Britain

Arguably, the Irish border that was made manifest between 1921 and 1925 was an imperial frontier because it was imposed by the British Empire in retreat (Anderson & O'Dowd, 2007). Eventually, the border began to resemble a state border through the UK shift from imperial power to national state, state-building in Sáorstat Éireann (Irish Free State), and the consolidation of a British unionist administration in Northern Ireland. However, the reconfiguration of the Irish border from imperial frontier to state border remained partial. The Common Travel Area between Britain and Ireland may be understood as an imperial residue of the UK state and a symbol of Ireland's neo-colonial dependency on Britain.[15] A benign understanding of the Common Travel Area is that it enables freedom of movement for British and Irish citizens between Britain and Ireland. In effect, however, freedom of movement in the Common Travel Area has been predicated on the coordination of immigration policies operated by the UK and Ireland to secure what was called the 'common outer perimeter' of the isles of Britain and Ireland (Meehan, 2014).

Despite the formation of the Sáorstat Éireann in 1921 and its exit from the Commonwealth in 1949, citizens of the 'Free State' (to 1937) and then of the Republic of Ireland (from 1949) retained the legal right to enter Britain and avail of the same rights as British citizens. Echoes of this British imperial consciousness reverberated in Section 2 of the UK's 1949 Ireland Act: 'Notwithstanding that the Republic of Ireland is not part of His Majesty's Dominions, the Republic of Ireland is not a foreign country for the purposes of any law in force in any part of the UK' S. 2 (1).[16] The 1949 Ireland Act remains in force.

This did not mean that the common travel area was insulated from higher security concerns. In response to security threats 'bordering Britain' was triggered without a qualm. In 1940 travellers from the island of Ireland were required to carry passports or limited travel documents for 'war-work' in order to enter Britain. A common travel area between Britain and Ireland was not reinstated fully until 1952 (Meehan, 2000, p. 26). In 1974, the introduction of the Prevention of Terrorism (Temporary Provisions) Act gave the British Home Secretary the power to prevent individuals moving from Northern Ireland to Britain and also to deport individuals from Britain to Northern Ireland:

If the Secretary of State is satisfied that

(a) any person (whether in Great Britain or elsewhere) is concerned in the commission, preparation or instigation of acts of terrorism, or

(b) any person is attempting or may attempt to enter Great Britain with a view to being concerned in the commission, preparation or instigation of acts of terrorism,

the Secretary of State may make an order against that person prohibiting him from being in, or entering, Great Britain.[17]

Passengers at the 'Belfast Gate' of Britain's airports were familiar with the intrusion of border control paraphernalia decades before the experience became widespread after the drama of the 11 September 2001 Islamic jihadist attacks on the United States of America. Britain's border within the UK, combined with the permeability of the UK's land border with Ireland and Westminster's willingness to allow Northern Ireland to secede unilaterally (unlike Scotland or Wales) in the event of a majority in Northern Ireland approving such a move, is thus problematic for the idea of a UK border that is coterminous with the UK state. Britain is the de facto state and its borders are 'fuzzy' (Rose, 1983, pp. 31–32).

A Brexit quest to secure borders and identify and exclude unwanted outsiders raises the issue of whether Ireland is to be regarded as a 'foreign country'. If the answer is 'yes' then the continued existence of the Common Travel Area between Britain and Ireland is called into question. However, a Brexit border security regime may also exclude Northern Ireland given the economic expense, practical difficulties and political risks involved in attempting to secure the Irish border. In a Brexit bordered Britain passengers travelling from Ireland to Britain would be required to produce some form of identification at ports and airports in order to be processed in the British border control system and gain entry into Britain. Travellers departing from Northern Ireland to Britain would receive the same treatment given the porous nature of the Irish border.

This would mean that Britain's border portals (at ports and airports) would become the foci for Brexit securitisation. The requirement to produce a form of identification other than a passport at a Britain's border security portal checkpoints would help to soothe Ulster British national identity sensitivities. Brexit's totemic 'bring back control' of immigration and the disbarment of unwanted outsiders from Britain indicates that the performance of such checks would have to take place at Britain's border portals in any case. Passing the burden of immigration restriction wholly to employers, landlords and the education sector is unlikely to satisfy the controlling urges of Brexiters.

This 'Bordering Britain' option is attractive on three counts: firstly, it would honour a cross-border, cross-community democratic wish articulated in the oft repeated refrain in the political domain, namely, 'no one wants to see a hard border' on the island of Ireland; secondly, it would be practically easier and economically less costly to establish and manage and thirdly, it would avoid the risk of a return to the violence associated with a hard Irish border, as noted by the PSNI's Deputy Chief Constable.[18] As Kapka Kassabova accurately observes, 'an actively policed border is always aggressive: it is where power suddenly acquires a body, if not a human face, and an ideology' (2017, p. xvi). In the case of the Irish border, bordering requires bodies with (concealed) human faces that would re-dramatise the conflicting British and Irish nationalist ideologies that two decades of debordering have helped to ameliorate.

The logic of Brexit is that Britain's borders may well retreat to Britain, and possibly to England and Wales thereafter, in the quest to render them, clear, secure and impenetrable to unwanted outsiders. Such bordering would reflect the British national imagination. Though the Scottish imagined community may demur, the British national imagination has the borders of the UK fixed firmly on Britain—This Sceptred Isle. Political psychologists have found that, in the British context, 'allusions to the geographical boundaries of imagined community [the island] may be used as a substitute for reference to the common and distinctive character or "identity" of the population' (Abell et al., 2006). 'This Sceptred Isle' and the 'White Cliffs of Dover' pervade heroic, romantic and (banal) nationalist readings of British history (Billig, 1995). Popular television and radio programmes such as the 10-week BBC Radio 4 series *This Sceptred Isle*, the long-running BBC comedy *Dad's Army*, as well as its seemingly endless documentary series *Coast* have helped to inculcate an idea of Britain in the British communal imagination. This Sceptred Isle—from Land's End to John O'Groats—remains the key reference point for Britain, British identity and the 'British way of life'.

Northern Ireland does not feature on this 'mainland' British radar. When British broadcasters announced the inclusion of seven political parties—Conservative, Labour, Liberal Democrat, UKIP, SNP, Green and Plaid Cymru—in the line-up for the 2015 General Election televised debates, Northern Ireland parties were overlooked. When the then Democratic Unionist Party (DUP) leader, Peter Robinson, complained that his party was the fourth largest at Westminster and should, therefore, be included, he was rebuffed by the BBC's Director General, Tony Hall, on the grounds that the party political structure in Northern Ireland differs significantly from the rest of the UK.[19] In his effort to avoid the debates altogether the then Prime Minister David Cameron cited the initial exclusion of the Greens, not the DUP, as grounds for his non-participation.

According to Elizabeth Meehan, 'Great Britain being an island is still crucial to the outlooks of governments on the maintenance of frontier controls' (2000, p. 60). British public opinion reflects the position of UK Governments on Britain's borders. In an ICM opinion poll published in the *Guardian* newspaper on 21 August 2001, the question posed to a sample of Britons in Britain was:

> Do you think Northern Ireland should be part of the UK? 26 per cent responded that it should remain part of the UK, 41 per cent that it should be joined with Ireland, and 33 per cent responded 'don't know'.[20]

Needless to say, unionists in Northern Ireland do not share that outlook. Arlene Foster (DUP, Leader) appeared to be aware of the possibility of Brexit bordering Britain when she declared: 'There must be no internal borders within the UK'[21]. After entering into a 'confidence and supply' supportive arrangement with the post-2017 General Election minority Conservative government it appeared that the DUP's opposition to bordering Britain was shorn up by that government. Its Department for Exiting the EU rejected the idea of locating Brexit customs controls at ports and airports stating 'we cannot create a Border between Northern Ireland and Great Britain' (Staunton, 2017). Yet, Phase 1 negotiations on Brexit entertained the option of ports and airports in Britain and Northern Ireland becoming the foci for customs and border inspections that would ensure the integrity of the Single Market, to which Northern Ireland would be 'fully aligned'. A non-tariff deal between the Northern Ireland Executive and the UK Government on Irish goods entering Britain also remained a possibility. Arguably, this scenario is intimated in the linguistic contortions of the 'Joint report from the negotiators of the European Union and the United Kingdom Government on progress during phase 1 of negotiations under Article 50 TEU on the United Kingdom's orderly withdrawal from the European Union' (European Commission, 8 December 2017, paragraphs 49 and 50). Such a scenario would avoid the economic damage of a hard Irish border to integrated sectors on the island, notably the agri-food sector. In any case, state security checks on bodies with human faces entering Britain through its ports and airports remained beyond the pale of these negotiations, even though freedom of movement of EU workers was a key driver of Brexit.

Option 3: Bordering the Isles of Britain and Ireland

As the operation of the Common Travel Area testifies, a high level of cooperation and information sharing between the UK and Irish electronic border control systems is evident and could form the basis for the development of a hard border around the isles of Britain and Ireland. In terms of intelligence and state security, it may be assumed that information sharing between relevant Intelligence agencies in Britain and Ireland is already highly developed.

Brexit raises the possibility of an intensification of UK–Ireland security cooperation to the ends of bordering the isles of Britain and Ireland and excluding unwanted outsiders, including non-Irish EU citizens. However, such a course of action would present the Irish Government with serious questions, not least one regarding Ireland's continued membership of the EU. Any attempt to restrict the mobility of EU workers runs counter to the EU's freedom of movement of labour principle contained in the *Acquis Communautaire*. This did not stop most pre-2004 member states, including France and Germany, from imposing their own temporary restrictions on workers from the 2004 Enlargement states: restrictions can be maintained for a maximum of seven years after accession. The difference is that the proposition of UK–Ireland bordering to control freedom of movement of people suggests the imposition of permanent restrictions. Such an eventuality would position Ireland for an 'Irexit'.

In the context of Treaty of Lisbon (2009), Hugo Brady, Centre for European Reform, claimed that: 'Following on from Ireland's decision to follow London and opt out of key parts of the reform treaty, it increasingly looks like Ireland is a small country latched to Britain like a koala on justice [and home affairs] issues ... '[22]. However, leaving the EU is an entirely different proposition for a small state like Ireland that has been unremittingly committed to EU membership principles, reaping 40 years of benefits in terms of acquiring sovereignty, developing infrastructurally, and opening culturally[23] (Laffan & O'Mahony, 2008). Moreover, as the former British Labour MP and Minister for Europe, Denis Mac-Shane, has pointed out, Brexit would absolve the UK government from the obligation to treat Ireland with the status, respect and reciprocity that it acquired upon both states becoming EC member states in 1973 (MacShane, 2015, p. 20). An 'Irexit' would further expose Ireland to the vagaries of British politics in a new asymmetrical relationship with its much larger and more powerful neighbour. On the possibility of an Irexit, a former Taoiseach (Irish Prime Minister) commented: 'we're mad, but we're not that mad'.[24]

Conclusion

During the Northern Ireland 'Troubles', the political risks of a continuous and 'seamless' (in the security barrier sense) Irish border were recognised by the British Government. That border has undergone a 20 year reconfiguration—driven by Europeanisation, the North South provisions of the Good Friday Agreement and an avalance of cross-border cooperation initiatives—that has rendered it open and free flowing for unhindered mobility, contact, communication, cooperation and trade.

The Brexit campaign was primarily concerned with 'bringing back control' of the movement of unwanted 'outsiders' to Britain, including EU citizens from mainland Europe. Bordering is the principal mechanism for asserting such control. Therefore, the key Brexit question is: Where to implement bordering? This paper has explored three options: bordering the United Kingdom of Great Britain and Northern Ireland; bordering Britainand bordering the isles of Britain and Ireland.

In the context of the Irish border, Brexit raised the possibility of border checkpoints on main arterial routes, hundreds of secondary cross-border road closures, and mobile border security patrols to control the movement of people and goods across it. However, the economic cost, practical difficulties and political risks in doing so mean that other options are worthy of exploration. An alternative option would be to hard border the isles of Britain and Ireland. Heretofore, the Irish Government has followed the UK Government on justice and home affairs issues. Such evidence suggests that Ireland could follow Britain's lead in hardening an isles of Britain and Ireland border zone. However, such a course of action would jeopardise Ireland's EU membership because it would present an affront to the EU's primary freedom of movement of labour principle. Furthermore, 'Irexit' would expose a small state to the vagaries of its asymmetrical relationship with a large and powerful neighbour devoted to seeking new economic and political relationships around the globe. From the perspective of Ireland, membership of the EC/EU has helped to calibrate the British–Irish relationship and protect Ireland's interests making the proposition of an Irexit 'mad'.

The least-worse option is to border Britain. The border of Britain is the UK border in the British national imagination. The border of Britain is an imagined border that is disseminated by the British media, endorsed by the political establishment, and is reflected in the British public attitudes. There are historical precedents for bordering Britain. This option would be problematic for the DUP in Northern Ireland and, potentially, for the Irish peace process if perceptions of Ulster British abandonment took hold. However, it would be relatively simple to establish and cause least disruption given the fact that border portals—ports and airports—are already sites of identity checking and border security regimes. Post-Brexit, bordering Britain for bodies with human faces is likely to happen regardless of the bordering option that is officially endorsed.

Acknowledgements

The author thanks John Coakley, Liam O'Dowd and, Special Issue Editor, Etain Tannam, who each commented on earlier drafts of this paper.

Funding

The author acknowledges the support of the research project EUBORDERSCAPES (290775), 2012–2016, which was funded by the European Commission under the 7th Framework Programme (FP7-SSH-2011-1), Area 4.2.1: The evolving concept of borders.

Notes

1. The Special EU Programmes Body (SEUPB) manages EU programmes including Interreg and the EU Peace Programmes.
2. The latter at the border crossing between Ballyconnell, County Cavan (Ireland) and Derrylin, County Fermanagh (Northern Ireland). See http://www.irishnews.com/news/brexit/2017/12/08/news/brexit-border-assurances-are-politically-bulletproof-says-taoiseach-leo-varadkar-1206145/ (accessed 08/12/2017).
3. *Irish Times*, 10 September 2009 (accessed 10/07/2017).
4. The 'Brexit Europeans' support for the free movement of capital and commodities across the EU is in stark contrast to their objections to the free of movement of labour. Therein lies an inherent contradiction since there is an inevitable connection between market integration and the free movement of labour to service that market in the neo-liberal economic model.
5. See, for example, http://www.express.co.uk/news/uk/566380/Britain-braces-more-immigrants-Calais-refugee-camp-Sangatte-2 and http://www.dailymail.co.uk/news/article-2174296/The-return-Sangatte-Inside-new-mini-migrant-camp-close-Calais.html (both accessed 23/06/2016).
6. http://www.bbc.co.uk/news/uk-politics-33716501 (accessed 04/06/2016).
7. http://press.conservatives.com/post/98882674910/david-cameron-speech-to-conservative-party (accessed 02/01/2016).
8. At bbc.co.uk/news/uk-politics-26960905 (accessed 04/08/2016).
9. Gibraltar shares a land border with Spain. However, under the Treaty of Rome (1973) and the UK Act of Accession (1973) Gibraltar is classified as a dependent territory of the UK and not as a member of the UK.
10. *Financial Times*, 25 July 2016 (accessed 28/07/2017).
11. The EU, being a customs union, requires border customs posts to be established between the EU and non-members. This is the case between the EU and Norway which is the subject of the most advanced EU free trade agreement with a non-member state.
12. Such roads connect border cities, towns and villages including Derry, Strabane, Lifford, Pettigo, Belleek, Belcoo, Blacklion, Swanlinbar, Aghalane, Belturbet, Newtownbutler, Clones, Aughnacloy, Middletown, Dundalk and Newry.
13. The Institute also proposed transforming the SEUPB into a border security agency, post-Brexit (Singham et al., 2017, p. 8).
14. *Irish Times*, 11 April 2016. At http://www.irishtimes.com/news/ireland/irish-news/brexit-could-lead-to-irish-border-controls-tories-warn-1.2605627 (accessed 22/08/2016).
15. Elizabeth Meehan has pointed out that The Common Travel Area was referred to as 'the common travel area' in policy documents before it became The Common Travel Area through international recognition bestowed on it by the 1997 Treaty of Amsterdam (2000, p. 1).
16. http://www.legislation.gov.uk/ukpga/Geo6/12-13-14/41 (accessed 10/02/2017).
17. Part II Exclusion Orders, 3:3, *Prevention of Terrorism (Temporary Provisions) Act 1974* at http://cain.ulst.ac.uk/hmso/pta1974.htm (accessed 19/05/2017).

18. See https://www.newsletter.co.uk/news/crime/post-brexit-border-infrastructure-obvious-target-for-dissid ent-republican-terrorists-1-8280713 (accessed 08/12/2017).
19. http://www.bbc.co.uk/news/uk-politics-31029232 (accessed 04/06/2016).
20. There has not been a similar poll conducted since 2001. However, there are no indicators to suggest that the percentages revealed in the 2001 poll have shifted significantly in the interim.
21. *Financial Times*, 25 July 2016 (accessed 28/07/2017).
22. www.cer.org.uk/articles/52_brady.html (accessed 06/12/2016).
23. The implications of Brexit for the island of Ireland alarmed the Irish Government. For example, in a speech at Queen's University, Belfast on 4 August 2017, the Irish Taoiseach (Prime Minister) Leo Varadkar highlighted the challenges of Brexit for the island of Ireland, particularly those relating to the Irish border (Garry, 2017). There have also been a number of Irish scholarly interventions on the subject. See, for example, Kilcourse (2013), O'Ceallaigh and Kilcourse (2013), and O'Ceallaigh and Gillespie (2015).
24. Bertie Ahern in the *Independent*, 28 July 2017 at http://www.independent.co.uk/news/world/europe/ ireland-bertie-ahern-brexit-britain-leave-eu-european-union-mad-republic-southern-irish-prime- a7864556.html (accessed 20/08/2017).

References

Abell, J., Condor, S., & Stevenson, C. (2006). 'We are an Island': Geographical imagery in accounts of citizenship, civil society and national identity in Scotland and England. *Political Psychology*, 27(2), 207–226.

Amilhat Szary, A.-L., & Giraut, F. (2015). Borderities: The politics of contemporary mobile borders. In A.-L. A. Szary & F. Giraut (Eds.), *Borderities and the politics of contemporary mobile borders* (pp. 1–19). Basingstoke: Palgrave Macmillan.

Amoore, L. (2006). Biometric borders: Governing mobilities in the war on terror. *Political Geography*, 25(3), 336–351.

Anderson, J., & O'Dowd, L. (2007). Imperial disintegration and the creation of the Irish border: Imperialism and nationalism 1885-1925. *Political Geography*, 26(8), 295–308.

Anderson, M., with Bort, E. (2001). *The frontiers of the European Union*. Basingstoke: Macmillan.

Andreas, P. (2003). Redrawing the line: Borders and security in the twenty-first century. *International Security*, 28(2), 78–111.

Berezin, M. (2003). Territory, emotion and identity. In M. Berezin & M. Schain (Eds.), *Europe without borders: Remapping territory, citizenship and identity in a transnational age* (pp. 1–30). Baltimore: John Hopkins University.

Billig, M. (1995). *Banal nationalism*. London: Sage.

Broeders, D. (2011). A European 'border' surveillance system under construction. In D. Huub & M. Albert (Eds.), *Migration and new technological borders of Europe* (pp. 40–67). Basingstoke: Palgrave Macmillan.

Buzan, B. (1993). State security and internationalization. In W. Ole, B. Barry, K. Morten, & L. Pierre (Eds.), *Identity, migration and the new security agenda in Europe* (pp. 41–58). London: Pinter.

Coakley, J., Ó Caoindealbháin, B., & Wilson, R. (2007). Institutional cooperation: The north-south implementation bodies. In C. John & O. Liam (Eds.), *Crossing the border: New relationships between Northern Ireland and the Republic of Ireland* (pp. 31–60). Dublin: Irish Academic Press.

European Commission. (2017). *Joint report from the negotiators of the European Union and the United Kingdom Government on progress during phase 1 of negotiations under Article 50 TEU on the United Kingdom's orderly withdrawal from the European Union* (8 December 2017), TF50 (2017) 19—Commission to EU 27. Retrieved from https://ec.europa.eu/commission/publications/joint-report-negotiators-european-union- and-united-kingdom-government-progress-during-phase-1-negotiations-under-article-50-teu-united- kingdoms-orderly-withdrawal-european-union_en

Garry, J. (2017, August 4). Leo Varadkar: Irish leader reveals fraying patience over Brexit border. *The Conversation*. Retrieved from http://theconversation.com/leo-varadkar-irish-leader-reveals-fraying-patience-over- brexit-border-82099

Häkli, J. (2015). The border in the pocket: The passport as a boundary object. In A.-L. A. Szary & F. Giraut (Eds.), *Borderities and the politics of contemporary mobile borders* (pp. 85–99). Basingstoke: Palgrave Macmillan.

Kassabova, K. (2017). *Border: A journey through the edge of Europe*. London: Granta Books.

Keating, M. (2004). European integration and the nationalities question. *Politics & Society*, 32(3), 367–388.

Keating, M. (2010). *The government of Scotland: Public policy making after devolution*. Edinburgh: Edinburgh University Press.

Keating, M. (2016, July 2). Where next for a divided United Kingdom?. *The Irish Times*.

Kilcourse, J. (2013, November 6). Ireland raises its voice in the UK's EU debate. *IIEA Blog*. Retrieved from www.iiea.com/blogosphere/ireland-raises-its-voice-in-the-uks-eu-debate

Kolossov, V. (2005). Border studies: Changing perspectives and theoretical approaches. *Geopolitics, 10*(4), 606–632.

Laffan, B., & O'Mahony, J. (2008). *Ireland and the European Union*. Basingstoke: Palgrave Macmillan.

Laffan, B., & Payne, D. (2001). *Creating living institutions: EU programmes after the Good Friday Agreement*. Armagh: Centre for Cross Border Studies.

Leary, P. (2016). *Unapproved routes: Histories of the Irish border 1922-1972*. Oxford: Oxford University Press.

Liddle, R. (2015). *The risk of Brexit: Britain and Europe in 2015*. London: Rowan and Littlefield.

MacShane, D. (2015). *Brexit: How Britain will leave Europe*. London: I.B. Tauris.

McCall, C. (2011). Culture and the Irish border: Spaces for conflict transformation. *Cooperation and Conflict, 46* (2), 201–221.

McCall, C. (2014). *The European Union and peacebuilding: The cross-border dimension*. Basingstoke: Palgrave Macmillan.

Meehan, E. (2000). *Free movement between Ireland and the UK: From the 'common travel area' to the common travel area*. Dublin: The Policy Institute.

Meehan, E. (2014). Borders and boundaries: The Irish example. *Centre on Constitutional Change blogspot*. Retrieved fromhttp://www.centreonconstitutionalchange.ac.uk/blog/borders-and-boundaries-irish-example

Nash, C., Reid, B., & Graham, B. (2013). *Partitioned lives: The Irish borderlands*. Farnham: Ashgate.

O'Ceallaigh, D., & Gillespie, P. 2015. *Britain and Europe: The endgame*. Dublin: The Institute of International and European Affairs.

O'Ceallaigh, D., & Kilcourse, J. (2013). *Untying the Knot: Ireland, the UK and the EU*. Dublin: The Institute of International and European Affairs.

O'Dowd, L. (2002). The changing significance of European borders. *Regional and Federal Studies, 12* (4), 13–36.

Patterson, H. (2013). *Ireland's violent frontier: The border and Anglo-Irish relations during the troubles*. Basingstoke: Palgrave Macmillan.

Peoples, C., & Williams, N. V. (2015). *Critical security studies: An introduction*. London: Routledge.

Phinnemore, D., & McGowan, L. (2013). *A dictionary of the European Union*. London: Routledge.

Pollak, S. (2016, January 11). Search after young man's death bonds border communities. *The Irish Times*.

Rose, R. (1983). *Is the United Kingdom a state?* Glasgow: Centre for the Study of Public Policy.

Ruane, J., & Todd, J. (2001). The politics of transition? Explaining political crises in the implementation of the Belfast Good Friday Agreement. *Political Studies, 49*, 923–940.

Singham, S., Morgan, A., Hewson, V., & Brooks, A. (2017). *How the UK and EU can resolve the Irish border issue after Brexit* (p. 28). London: Legatum Institute. Retrieved from http://www.li.com/activities/publications/mutual-interest-how-the-uk-and-eu-can-resolve-the-irish-border-issue-after-brexit.

Sørensen, G. (1999). Sovereignty: Change and continuity in a fundamental institution. *Political Studies, 47*, 590–604.

Staunton, D. (2017, July 29). UK Rules out moving border to Irish sea. *The Irish Times*.

Taylor, C. (2017, August 16). Post-Brexit tech border deemed 'complete nonsense' by IT experts. *The Irish Times*. Retrieved fromhttp://www.irishtimes.com/business/technology/post-brexit-tech-border-deemed-complete-nonsense-by-it-experts-1.3188475

van Houtum, H., & Pijpers, R. (2007). The European Union as a gated community: The two-faced border and immigration regime of the EU. *Antipode, 39*(2), 291–309.

Vaughan-Williams, N. (2009). *Border politics: The limits of sovereign power*. Edinburgh: Edinburgh University Press.

Waever, O. (1995). Securitization and desecuritization. In R. D. Lipschutz (Ed.), *On security* (pp. 46–86). New York, NY: Columbia University Press.

Wallace, W. (1999). The sharing of sovereignty: The European paradox. *Political Studies, XLVII*(3), 503–521.

Walsh, D. (2011). Police cooperation across the Irish border: Familiarity breeding contempt for transparency and accountability. *Journal of Law and Society, 38* (2), 301–330.

Walters, W. (2006). Border/control. *European Journal of Social Theory, 9*(2), 187–203.

The British–Irish Relationship in the Twenty-first Century

JOHN COAKLEY

ABSTRACT   The twentieth anniversary of the Good Friday agreement offers a useful vantage point from which to review the agreement's progress, particularly because the anniversary coincides with Brexit, a process likely to place it under particular strain. Using both evidence offered elsewhere in this collection and new material, this article reviews the two decades since the agreement in 1998 using as a framework the three relationships that the agreement sought to address. First, it argues that a combination of structural reform, social change, demographic transformation and political reconfiguration has substantially removed the incentives for inter-communal conflict in Northern Ireland, though without completely eliminating overt political violence, as worrying indicators of dissent survive. Second, it contends that the provisions of the agreement for the promotion of institutionalised cooperation between Northern Ireland and the Republic have had limited impact, but that they have been supplemented by new forms of all-Ireland integration driven by change at EU level. Third, the article suggests that the once-hostile relationship between the Republic of Ireland and the United Kingdom has mellowed, a change that both facilitated the settlement of 1998 and was itself reinforced by this. The article concludes that the institutions established by the Good Friday agreement have had a mixed impact, and that they face a particular challenge in the context of the UK's withdrawal from the EU.

Introduction

In the run-up to the UK's departure from the EU, there was no shortage of warnings about the implications of Brexit for peace on the island of Ireland. Stevenson (2017, p. 111), for example, argued that, with their focus on continental Europe, Brexiteers 'overlooked a conflict not yet fully resolved—and a peace not yet fully consolidated—at home', that associated with the Good Friday agreement of 1998. Other researchers made similar points (Doyle & Connolly, 2017; O'Leary, 2018; Phinnemore & Hayward, 2017; Soares, 2016). This perspective was echoed in a report commissioned by the European Parliament, which warned that 'prospects for a bespoke, tariff-free Northern Ireland-EU cross-border trade arrangement appear slim, whilst a continuing Common Travel Area is in jeopardy', with big implications for Ireland's relationship with the UK, and for the 1998 agreement in particular (Tonge, 2017, p. 11). Not surprisingly, then, the EU Commission gave a central position to the Irish question in the first phase of negotiations, and the report of the negotiators devoted 15 out of its 96 paragraphs to this, acknowledging that the Good Friday agreement 'must be protected in all its parts' (EU Commission, 2017, para. 42).

Recognition of the crucial importance of the agreement raises big questions about its standing at the point at which it is coming under pressure from the UK–EU negotiations, a consideration that is the focus of the articles in this collection. Twenty years after its adoption, to what extent has the Good Friday agreement demonstrated its pivotal position by delivering on its early promise of reducing the intensity of Northern Ireland's historic enmities and resolving the troubled British–Irish relationship? The present article seeks to assess the impact of the agreement by looking at the evolution of key areas from the 1990s, when the agreement was reached, to the present, as the British–Irish relationship takes a new and more unpredictable turn. In doing so, it makes sense to revert to the three strands that were defined as core components in the conflict that the agreement sought to address: inter-communal relations and domestic political institutions within Northern Ireland, relationships between political leaders (and their followers) in Northern Ireland and the Republic, and the relationship between the two islands. The article reviews these three dimensions by taking into account the findings of the other articles in this collection, supplementing them by further analysis of areas not covered in these.

Nationalism and Unionism in a New Northern Ireland

The first big question to be addressed has to do with the manner in which the relationship between the two communities in Northern Ireland has been transformed in the demographic, socio-economic and political domains, as the level of violence has fallen. A useful benchmark for assessing political relationships in contemporary Northern Ireland may be found by going back not to the years immediately before the Good Friday agreement, but to the period more than 30 years earlier, before the eruption of the initial civil rights protests (for background, see O'Leary & McGarry, 1996; Ruane & Todd, 1996; Tonge, 2002). One of the early civil rights activists, Con McCluskey, described in stark terms the position in the 1960s in his own town of Dungannon, equally divided between Catholics and Protestants, and a microcosm of Northern Ireland:

> There were two textile factories, both Protestant owned, and the upper echelons of the workforce were virtually all Protestant. The larger shops were mainly Protestant owned and staffed. A few Catholic owners were in business in a smaller way. The best and largest farms were owned by Protestants. There were four Protestant banks and one Catholic. Protestants dominated the health services and the hospital, the Ministry of Labour, Post Office and Electricity Board. Most lower-status nurses, lesser artisans and labourers were Catholic. ... Catholics were inferior creatures and felt themselves to be 'second class citizens'. (McCluskey, 1989, p. 9)

These objective and subjective markers of inferior socio-economic standing were matched by marginal political status. Enjoying an enormous and stable majority in the Northern Ireland House of Commons and a monopoly of ministerial appointments, the Unionist Party was able to ignore pleas and complaints from the nationalist minority, resulting in a form of politics that has variously been described as 'majority dictatorship' (with uninterrupted single-party rule, though based on a continuing electoral majority) and 'crystalised politics' (with the dominant party effectively empowered to ignore all other groups, and disposed to do so) (Arthur, 1974, pp. 11–13).

As is well known, the transformation of Northern Ireland was a bitter and painful process, marked by violence, conflict and civil unrest. Its trajectory as measured by deaths arising from civil unrest is a familiar one: a sudden upsurge in the early 1970s, followed by a reduction from 1977 onwards, but still with about 100 deaths per year. Figure 1 takes up the story from 1990 to 2017. This shows a sharp fall in the number of deaths in 1994, the year of the IRA and loyalist ceasefires, but an upsurge in 1998 as a consequence of the Omagh bombing. The death rate subsequently was very low, with an average of two per year from 2008 onwards. But this is not the full story: Figure 1 also reports the level of paramilitary-related injuries and shooting incidents. Here, the notable drop was in 2006, perhaps related to the accelerating pace of political dialogue in that year.

While the Good Friday agreement led to a big reduction in political violence, then, its effects were not immediate: the decline in levels of violence began before that date, and violence continued after it. Other aspects of the steady emergence of social and political 'normality' are recorded in a series of comprehensive analyses sponsored by the Community Relations Commission (Nolan, 2012, 2013, 2014; Wilson, 2016). These concluded that while the new institutions had bedded down and there was wider acceptance of Northern Ireland's diversity, serious areas of concern remained. The most important of these were a continuing paramilitary threat, the absence of a reconciliation strategy and of mechanisms for dealing with the past, the impact of economic recession and the new challenges posed by Brexit, and growing problems of alienation, especially on the part of young Protestant men. Ironically, it seems that although Catholics continue to fare worse than Protestants on almost all measures of social deprivation, the rise of the Catholic middle class and the predominance of Catholics in higher education have had the effect of unsettling Protestants,

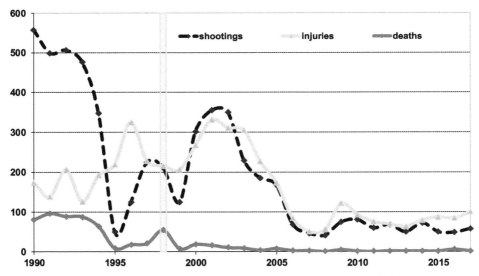

Figure 1. Indicators of paramilitary-related activity, 1990–2017.
Note: The vertical grey bar indicates the year of the Good Friday agreement.
Source: Computed from Police Service of Northern Ireland (2018a).

with disputes over the flying of flags acting as 'a lightning rod for such Protestant unease' (Nolan, 2014, p. 13). Educational underachievement among young Protestant working-class males is reflected in 'hyper-masculine confrontations with the police' and diffuse Protestant fears of the loss of 'Britishness' in Northern Ireland in the context of a 'culture war' of which Protestants perceive themselves as victims (Nolan, 2014, pp. 12–14). Public opinion data since 1998 show a broad decline in support for the agreement and its institutions and negative assessments of the Assembly's achievements, especially among Protestants—a shift attributable at least in part to a perception that Catholics had benefited more from the agreement (Hayes & McAllister, 2013, pp. 94–104). Overall, the weakness of the Northern Ireland economy, with its dependence on financial subvention from London, leaves the region particularly vulnerable to the consequences of Brexit (Bradley, 2018).

The big political changes in Northern Ireland are largely consequences of the negotiation process that led to the several political agreements. But they were accompanied by a steady convergence of the two communities in three crucial respects: replacement of the long-running majority–minority demographic relationship by one of parity; transition from inter-communal socio-economic inequality (in effect, a kind of ethnic division of labour) to substantial equality; and conversion of the political gap between nationalists and unionists into a more equal distribution of political resources between the two. This process has helped to undermine the sense of grievance that formed such an important ingredient in militant nationalist mobilisation; but it is not without negative consequences. These same changes are potentially unsettling for unionists, many of whom fear them as challenging their traditional position of dominance; and, as Bradley (2018) argues, many unionists have been prepared to vote with their hearts rather than with their heads in selecting their options for the future.

The route towards demographic parity between the two communities in Northern Ireland is a well-known one, even if its full extent and its political significance are imperfectly acknowledged in public debate. In brief, the denominational balance in early twentieth-century Northern Ireland (with Protestants outnumbering Catholics by a ratio of almost two to one) was sustained mainly by an above-average Catholic emigration rate. By the middle of the century, the Catholic rate of natural increase was much higher than the Protestant rate, and from 1971 onwards this was reflected in a growing Catholic share of the population (for details, see Coakley, 2016, 2018a). This was reinforced by gradual alignment of the Catholic and Protestant emigration rates. There was clear evidence around the turn of the century that Protestants were disproportionately likely to migrate to study in British universities, though evidence of a Protestant 'brain drain' remains inconclusive (McQuaid & Hollywood, 2008, pp. 6–10; Schubotz, 2008, pp. 15–16). By 2011, as may be seen in Figure 2, Catholics (by community background) outnumbered Protestants in all age cohorts below 40. By 2021, assuming continuation of this trend, this will mean an excess of Catholics over Protestants in all age cohorts below 50, and the numbers of Catholics and Protestants by community background will be substantially the same (about 46% each, with 8% in the 'other' category). Since these estimates are based on conservative assumptions, indeed, the proportion of Catholics is likely actually to be higher.[1]

One of the more intractable aspects of the early reform process in Northern Ireland was the difficulty of translating legislation designed to secure equality before the law into the reality of equality in the population and in the workplace. Structural inequalities inherited from the nineteenth century and earlier were carried over into the new Northern Ireland, and were in certain respects sustained and reinforced by discriminatory practices in the new

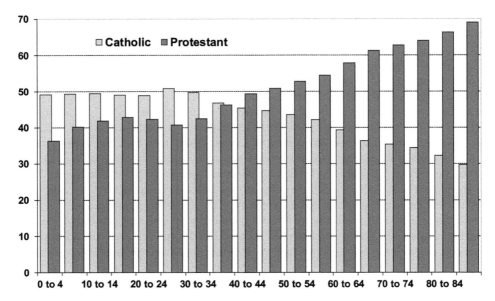

Figure 2. Population by community background and age cohort, 2011.
Note: Data refer to religion or (for those where this information was unavailable) religion in which brought up. The 'Other' category is not reported.
Source: Computed from Northern Ireland Statistics and Research Agency (2018).

state. The position in 1971 was described by Aunger (1975, p. 17) as comprising 'a noteworthy congruence between the class cleavage and the religious cleavage', one that impeded reconciliation between the communities. Inevitably, the first wave of reforms in Northern Ireland in 1969–1972 (tackling electoral law, local government, fair employment, housing, policing, community relations and other areas) had little immediate impact on economic inequalities, though of course laying the basis for a more equitable public culture in the future (Purdie, 1990, pp. 249–251). The introduction of direct rule from London in 1972 saw more assertive measures, notably the Fair Employment Act, 1976, charged with tackling discrimination and promoting equality of opportunity under the umbrella of a new Fair Employment Agency. But by the end of the 1980s, there were still striking Catholic–Protestant differences in employment and social status, suggesting that the earlier act had limited impact. Under political pressure from Irish American activists and the Irish government, revised legislation in 1989 provided for a more interventionist strategy, including monitoring of existing practices by a Fair Employment Commission, which replaced the earlier Agency in 1990. In a more comprehensive set of reforms as part of the Good Friday agreement, the legal position was further revamped and an Equality Commission with a far-reaching mandate took over in 1999 (Osborne & Shuttleworth, 2004).

These efforts to promote an equality agenda in the workplace gradually bore fruit, resulting in 'a more equitable distribution of employment' (Russell, 2004, pp. 47–48) and 'a strong equality regime which has significantly reduced communal economic inequality' (Todd, 2014, p. 532). The pattern of change has been identified as beginning with the Anglo-Irish agreement of 1985, which saw a shift in British policy 'from its alignment with unionists to a partnership with the Irish state and to a more even-handed stance in

Northern Ireland', a change 'of historic proportions, the breaking of the centuries-old geo-political alliance that had been a key component of the historic conflict' (Ruane & Todd, 2014, p. 23). The profile of change was dramatic, as Figure 3 shows. The top line reports the percentage of Catholics among the unemployed hovering stubbornly in the high 50s, and sometimes exceeding 60%, between 1992 and 2016. But since the proportion of Catholics in the working age population was increasing steadily at the same time, from 41% in 1990 to 44% in 2016 (43–52% if those for whom information on religious background was missing are excluded), this actually represented a narrowing of the unemployment gap between the two communities. Looked at differently, by 2016 the unemployment rates for Catholics and Protestants were 7% and 5%, respectively; the corresponding figures in 1992 were 18% and 9%, reflecting a long-term tendency for Catholics to have a much higher unemployment rate than Protestants. At the time of the 1981 census, the respective figures were 26% and 11% (Executive Office, 2018, p. 32; Osborne & Shuttleworth, 2004, p. 15).

Figure 3 also makes use of the employment monitoring reports that have been prepared since 1990 by the Equality Commission and its predecessor. These include all full-time public sector employees, and private sector employees in enterprises with at least 26 employees, amounting to an estimated 64–67% of all those in employment (the self-employed, those on government training schemes, school teachers and those working in

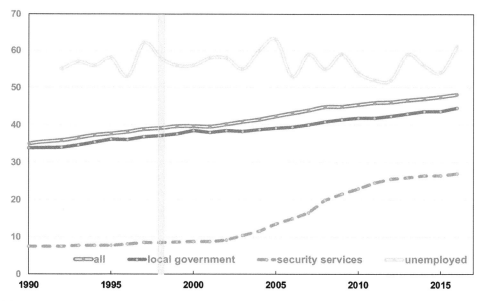

Figure 3. Catholics as percentage of unemployed, and in selected industrial categories, 1990–2016. *Note*: The vertical grey bar indicates the year of the Good Friday agreement. Data refer to Catholics by community background, or perceived community background, as percentage of all those whose background was known. The base for the unemployment data is the economically active population aged 16 years and over, and for the other measures the population of all monitored bodies (all public sector bodies, and private sector bodies with more than 25 employees).
Source: Computed from Executive Office (2018), and from Equality Commission for Northern Ireland (2002–2017), and associated excel tables (see www.equalityni.org/Delivering-Equality/Addressing-inequality/Employment/Monitoring-Report-27/Fair-Employment-Monitoring-Report-27).

small private sector concerns are not monitored; Equality Commission for Northern Ireland, 2017, p. 2).[2] It is noteworthy that over this period the proportion of Catholics in the monitored workforce has increased steadily, from 35% in 1990 to 48% in 2016 (see second line from the top in Figure 3). If this is broken down by industrial sectors, some interesting patterns emerge. The proportion of Catholics in the civil service, and the proportion in the monitored private sector, closely shadow the overall proportion of Catholics in the monitored workforce—so closely that it is not possible to illustrate them in this graph, as their profile overlaps almost completely with the overall pattern for the monitored workforce.[3] The percentage of Catholics employed by local authorities has been consistently below this (over the decade 2007–2016, it fell 3.7% points below the percentage of Catholics in the monitored workforce).

The big deviant is the security sector. The Patten report on policing, established under the terms of the agreement, had recommended in 1999 that, with a view to ensuring that the composition of the police service would match that of the population, a 50–50 ratio of Catholics to others would be recruited for a period of at least 10 years (Independent Commission on Policing for Northern Ireland, 1999, p. 88; see also Mulcahy, 2006, pp. 149–167). The British government decided, however, to let this practice lapse in 2011. The discussion paper that paved the way for this argued (accurately) that the proportion of Catholics had risen from 8% to 29% since 2001, and (inaccurately) that 'PSNI membership is now broadly representative of the community', leading the Secretary of State to conclude that the 50–50 recruitment ratio was no longer needed (Northern Ireland Office, 2010, pp. 2–3). As Figure 3 shows, the proportion of Catholics in the security services over all fell below 10% until 2003; following rapid growth until 2013, it stabilised, but had reached only 27% by 2016. In 2017, Catholic police officers made up 31.9% of those whose religious background was determined, but for civilian support staff, the corresponding figure was only 19.9% (computed from Police Service of Northern Ireland, 2018b). Thus, recruitment has not caught up with the growing Catholic share of the workforce; but the fact that policing arrangements are embedded in a wider compromise agreement helps to enhance their acceptability (Doyle, 2010, pp. 200–203).

The third area in which the relationship between the two communities in Northern Ireland has been transformed is the political one. By the mid-1960s, the old Nationalist Party held only nine seats out of the 52 in the Northern Ireland House of Commons. McCluskey (1989, p. 60) dismissed the party as 'entirely without drive, content to obtain minor favours for constituents from the various Unionist Governments'. Lynn (1997, p. 236) noted its dismal track record of achievement, with 'little to show in terms of advancing the cause of a united Ireland, or in significantly improving the lot of the minority community'. Staunton (2001, p. 310) described it as simply irrelevant—'a party obsessed with a border which Catholics felt should be talked about less'. The party's support was confined to rural Northern Ireland, with Belfast Catholics generally voting for a range of small left-leaning parties. But the replacement of this disorganised configuration of minority representatives by modern party vehicles—the Social Democratic and Labour Party in 1970, followed by Sinn Féin in the early 1980s—facilitated a growth in nationalist political power, and this was reinforced by the expanding Catholic electorate. At the same time, the unionist political monolith began to break apart, with the rise of the Democratic Unionist Party (DUP) and the fragmentation of the Ulster Unionist Party following the suspension of Stormont in 1972.

The broad political pattern over the past half-century is illustrated in Figure 4, which reports the relative strength of the two main blocs, and of those falling outside these, in

Stormont elections since 1965. Initial Unionist dominance was assisted by the plurality system used in Northern Ireland House of Commons elections up to 1969, but early elections under proportional representation (which was re-introduced in 1973) did not deliver a greatly different outcome. The big upsurge in combined nationalist electoral support dates from 1998, reflecting nationalist 'buy-in' to the Good Friday agreement, but also growing Catholic demographic weight, as discussed above. Indeed, in a dramatic development, unionists for the first time ever failed to win an overall majority in Stormont in 2017, following an election that reflected a sharply enhanced level of polarisation as a consequence of the events associated with the collapse of the power-sharing Executive in January 2017 (O'Leary, 2018). This new expression of nationalist electoral power reflected a transformation in the broader political resources available to the two communities. As the Northern Ireland conflict had become internationalised, traditional unionist reliance on its long-standing ally, the British government, had been challenged by diminishing British commitment to the unionist cause, an increasingly significant voice for the Irish government, and a growing interest on the part of the American government and the European Union—all developments that strengthened the negotiating position of the nationalist leadership (Todd, 2017).

Within Northern Ireland, then, there has been a substantial shift in the direction of parity between the two communities and a more even balance between them in respect of political power. The agreement has undoubtedly given political parties, and therefore the communities they represent, more proportionate access to political resources. That, after all, is precisely what the D'Hondt formula for allocation of seats on the Executive in proportion to members in the Assembly is designed to do, and it is reinforced by similar arrangements for the appointment of committee chairs, for the dual First Minister role and for such classic

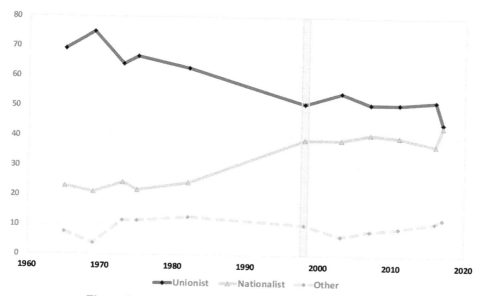

Figure 4. Seats won in Stormont elections by bloc, 1965–2017.
Note: The vertical grey bar indicates the year of the Good Friday agreement. The data refer to elections to the Northern Ireland House of Commons (1965–69), Assemblies (1973, 1982–2017) and Convention (1975).

consociational 'alarm-bell' procedures as petitions of concern and qualified majority voting.[4] It is clear that demographic change would have steadily eroded unionist dominance in any case, but the agreement provided a structured, near-consensual transition mechanism, one designed also to protect a future unionist minority.

The recalibration of the relationship between the two communities, however, has not been sufficient to ensure that all aspects of the agreement have been implemented. Remaining gaps include failure to adopt a promised bill of rights; non-enactment of an Irish language act (arguably implicit in the Anglo-Irish agreement of 1985 and the Good Friday agreement itself, but only explicitly agreed at St Andrews in 2006); and unresolved matters relating to dealing with the past and the display of flags. There have also been areas where the spirit of the agreement has been put under pressure. Thus, the adoption of modifying legislation to allow the formation of a parliamentary opposition in the Assembly in 2016 appears to run counter to conventional consociational principles, though it is not necessarily incompatible with them (see Matthews & Pow, 2017, pp. 321–322). Certainly, this reform failed to prevent the collapse of the devolved institutions in 2017, an episode that left Northern Ireland without an Executive at a critically important time in light of the Brexit debate, and one that seems to have contributed to a degree of popular disillusion with the operation of the political system.

What are the implications of Brexit for this most institutionally ambitious component of the agreement, strand one? A great deal of analysis stresses its obvious importance for Northern Ireland's external relations, both economic and political (Doyle & Connolly, 2017; Hayward & Phinnemore, 2018; Soares, 2016; Tonge, 2017). The fact that Northern Ireland was able to stagger along without an executive after January 2017 might be seen as implying that the devolved institutions are not essential to stability. This would be a dangerous conclusion, though, given the explicit interdependence of the major institutions established by the agreement. The compromise that the agreement represented rested on a trade-off between unionist and nationalist interests. The unspoken deal was that nationalists would in effect accept the status of Northern Ireland within the UK (though implicitly in the context of the UK's membership of the EU and explicitly with a right to take Northern Ireland out of the UK should a majority so wish), in return for access to political power within Northern Ireland. Unionists, in return, would accept the bicommunal character of Northern Ireland and the principle of equality between the two communities (with implications for cultural practices and symbolic issues that were not spelt out). The potential undermining of this compromise by the form taken by Brexit raises the risk of a reversion to paramilitary activity, especially in border areas, and renewal of wider inter-communal tensions. As Phinnemore and Hayward (2017, p. 50) warned, Brexit will 'symbolically and psychologically represent for many a reversal of the peace process and failure of the Good Friday agreement'.

The potential derailing of core features of the agreement poses particular difficulties for Sinn Féin, and therefore for the republican perspective more broadly, because of the radical compromise with traditional republican ideology that was entailed by that party's acceptance of the agreement. After all, this movement had come into existence in 1970 precisely because of dissatisfaction with the 'official' republican movement, which had allegedly been participating in a campaign 'to reform the Stormont parliament rather than seeking its abolition' (Devlin, 1993, p. 121). The IRA's initial military campaign targeted Stormont as an institution to be destroyed, not restructured. This remained a consistent Sinn Féin position. As late as four weeks before Good Friday 1998, party leader Gerry Adams was asserting the need for powerful all-Ireland institutions, arguing against 'an internal six county settlement' and dismissing 'any kind of new Stormont or any effort to underpin partition' as unacceptable (Adams, 1998). The settlement ultimately reached on Good Friday was thus far removed from the Sinn Féin position; as well as conflicting with the party's priorities on strands one and two, other Sinn Féin red lines identified by Adams were crossed, including the demand for recognition that 'the Irish people as a whole have a right to national self-determination', and that in any change to the Irish constitution 'the definition of the Irish national territory should not be diluted'. In this area, then, an enormous gulf between Sinn Féin and the other parties was bridged. For the DUP the ideological gap was smaller, though it took much longer than the other parties to accept the new arrangements.

In respect of their functioning, if account is taken of the long lead-in period in 1998–1999 and the two extended periods of suspension beginning in 2002 and 2017, the devolved institutions have been up and running for only 61% of the time since 1998 (a little more than 12 out of the 20 years). Furthermore, inter-party relations have been fractious, creating considerable difficulties in policy formation and provoking widespread public disillusion. The strand one institutions are least directly affected by Brexit, and they have notably failed to have a significant impact in defending Northern Ireland's interests in whatever the new post-Brexit political arrangements may be. Although the two first ministers were able to agree in July 2016 on a joint letter to the British prime minister putting Northern Ireland's case for a 'soft' border (Foster & McGuinness, 2016), a subsequent hardening of the DUP stance saw the party breaking with this position (a breach articulated most vociferously by the DUP MPs at Westminster), with attitudes towards Brexit becoming another source of major division between the two largest parties.

New Relationships Between North and South

One of the potentially most inflammatory areas addressed by the Good Friday agreement was the North–South relationship. By the end of the twentieth century, the priorities of northern unionism and southern nationalism on this relationship had been ironically reversed. Unionist leaders, prepared in the 1920s to accept the Council of Ireland provided for in the Government of Ireland Act, 1920, were now deeply suspicious of any institutionalised links with the South. Southern politicians, reluctant in the 1920s to have any truck with North–South bodies that were an uncomfortable reminder of partition, were now advocates of strong, formal North–South links. Indeed, such links, triggered by the Anglo-Irish agreement of 1985, had already been progressing at a modest level (Tannam, 2018).

Presented as a quid-pro-quo for devolution, the North–South dimension in the Good Friday agreement was pushed strongly by the nationalist side, against firm unionist resistance. But the unionist perspective was relatively pragmatic; as Bradley (2018) points out, unionists were sufficiently flexible to accommodate structures that would offer demonstrable advantages to both Northern Ireland and the Republic, and that would assist economic development. The EU context was vitally important in facilitating agreement on cross-border issues (Lagana, 2017). Hayward and Murphy (2018) argue that the European integration process had the effect of depoliticising and normalising North–South cooperation. But there were clear limits to unionist tolerance of any bridging of the border, driven both by concerns to protect Northern Irish identity (Bradley, 2018) and by pressure to defend Northern Ireland's position in respect of trade and competition for foreign direct investment (Tannam, 2018).

The final strand two package appeared to have the same political status as the strand one arrangements. While all of the institutions established by the Good Friday agreement were said to be 'interlocking and interdependent', there was a specific stipulation that 'the functioning of the Assembly and the North/South Council are so closely inter-related that the success of each depends on that of the other'. This rarely mentioned provision implies not only that collapse of the Assembly entails suspension of the Council but also that unsatisfactory functioning of the Council can prevent the functioning of the Assembly.

The North/South Ministerial Council normally meets in three formats, but did not meet at all during the periods when the devolved institutions in Belfast were suspended (February–May 2000, 2002–2007 and since January 2017). Of its meetings, 23 were plenaries (attended by the Taoiseach, First Minister, Deputy First Minister and most northern and southern ministers). Approximately a further 270 sectoral meetings have taken place (comprising the relevant southern minister, his or her northern counterpart, and a northern minister from the 'other' side). These originally rotated around the country, but from 2010 on took place mainly in Armagh, following the construction of a new headquarters building there. The Council has also met 10 times in 'institutional' format to discuss certain technical issues such as appointments to boards.

The six implementation bodies whose work is overseen by the North/South Ministerial Council were modest in scope, comprising a mixture of existing bodies that were reconstituted (such as the Foyle, Carlingford and Irish Lights Commission) and entirely new bodies (such as the Food Safety Promotion Board, now rebranded as Safefood, and InterTrade Ireland). Others had a hybrid status, made up of a mixture of existing agencies and new ones: the Language Body, for example, and Waterways Ireland. Alongside the implementation bodies were six 'areas of cooperation' where unspecified forms of joint action were to take place through existing departments, North and South (the areas are agriculture, education, environment, health, tourism and transport).

The North–South strand of the Good Friday agreement has proceeded with less fanfare than the institutions in Stormont, and has done nothing to stoke unionist fears that this might be a Trojan horse for Irish unity. Both the secretariat and the implementation bodies remain modest in size, and little expansion in their activities has taken place. It is true that a de-facto seventh body, Tourism Ireland, appeared in 2000, but this arose from long-running discussions that predated the Good Friday agreement. The number of employees of all seven bodies in 2003 was about 680, and this had risen only to 720 by 2016. At the same time, the combined budgets of these bodies actually fell, from €227m in 2003 to €116m in 2016 (though this was in part due to across-the-board Irish public sector cut-backs, and in any case it is difficult to make fully accurate comparisons over time, due to one-off start-up costs and other special activities or investments). At the same time, the permanent secretariat in Armagh fell from 27 people in 2003 to 18 in 2016 (derived from Coakley, 2005, p. 422, 2018b, p. 335).

Other planned North–South developments were slow to emerge. The Good Friday agreement had envisaged a joint parliamentary forum, bringing together members of the Assembly and of the Dáil and Seanad, but this finally took shape only in 2012, and then under the less ambitious designation of a North–South Inter-Parliamentary Association. By the time its most recent meeting took place on 2 December 2016, it had met on eight occasions. The agreement also envisaged 'an independent consultative forum appointed by the two Administrations, representative of civil society, comprising the social partners and other members with expertise in social, cultural, economic and other issues'; but, although the idea has not been formally dropped, little progress in establishing it can be recorded two decades after it was first put forward.

The limited impact of the strand two institutions does not, however, provide the full story of the North–South relationship. Many civil society organisations, such as trade unions, cultural associations and sporting organisations, had always been structured on an all-Ireland basis (Howard, 2007). The origins of certain agencies promoting collaboration in health and social care services, including Cooperation And Working Together (1992) and the Institute of Public Health in Ireland (1998), also predate the agreement (Pollak, 2017). A great deal of innovative North–South policy-making continued to proceed outside the terms of the agreement. Some of the most significant developments in the area of transport, for instance, took place during the period of direct rule, 2002–2007 (see Coakley & O'Dowd, 2007). It was during this period, too, that planning for the all-island single electricity market (integrating the northern and southern electricity supply systems) took place; the market itself came into existence in November 2007 (Gaffney, Deane, & Ó Gallachóir, 2017, p. 74). In areas like these, European Union intervention in promoting cross-border cooperation was central. Much of this took place within the framework of the agreement, notably through a new implementation body, the Special EU Programmes Body. But the EU role long predated the agreement, and some of its activities took place outside its parameters (see Murphy, 2014; Tannam, 1999).

Although the North/South Ministerial Council presented itself as a potentially useful vehicle for addressing the challenges of Brexit, the Irish government's most visible public response followed a different track: the launch of a series of meetings under the framework of an All-Island Civic Dialogue on Brexit. The meetings took place mainly in sectoral format, hosted by an individual minister (Department of the Taoiseach, 2017). Between 2 November 2016 and 30 April 2018, four plenary meetings involving civil society groups, business interests, cultural organisations, political parties and others had also taken place—a process resembling the proposed North–South civic forum, but taking place without reference to the terms of the Good Friday agreement. Apart from these meetings, the challenge posed by Brexit has had the effect of promoting more extensive North–South contact at civil service level (Tannam, 2018).

Any discussion of the North–South dimension must also take account of one potentially radical provision: the formula it offers for bringing about Irish unity in circumstances where this gains 'the consent of a majority of the people, democratically expressed' in both Northern Ireland and the Republic. The solidity of Protestant support for the union in Northern Ireland is, however, well known, and for the past decade surveys have suggested that Catholic support for Irish unity has been confined to a minority, so the likelihood of Irish unity as a consequence simply of demographic change is very low. Southern suggestions that the 50% (majority) support threshold for Irish unity in Northern Ireland would be insufficient to trigger change further highlighted the vulnerability of strand two of this component of the agreement.[5] Nevertheless, given the capacity of Brexit to disrupt existing geopolitical norms, the prospect has arisen of different types of 'bordering', with Northern Ireland's status and its relationship with the Republic of Ireland being potentially radically redefined (McCall, 2018).

Some of the most bitter battles during the peace negotiations focused on the range and powers of the strand two institutions. But the ultimate provisions of strand two were modest. Several of the North–South bodies were already in existence in another form, and the remainder were given limited competences. The areas of cooperation, though broadly defined by sector, had a very narrow subsectoral focus. The parliamentary tier appeared only in 2012, and no progress was made on establishing the consultative forum. Any notion that this set of institutions was the embryo of a united Ireland would have been misconceived; they were not animated by any dynamic resembling the kind of neofunctionalist pressures that drove European integration. The North/ South Ministerial Council might have served as a useful mechanism for formulating agreed positions on Brexit, and it carried out some valuable work in this area before it was brought down by the collapse of the Stormont institutions in 2017. The provisions of article 49 of the EU–UK agreement (EU Commission, 2017), which stipulate that 'in the absence of agreed solutions' the UK would take measures to 'support North-South cooperation, the all-island economy and the protection of the 1998 agreement', have particular significance. Given the limited remit of the North–South bodies provided for in the agreement, though, the strong argument against a 'hard' border is not the protection of these bodies, but safeguarding the other two areas, North–South cooperation and the all-island economy.

Normalisation of the British–Irish Relationship

While strand two of the agreement sought to address an exceptional challenge (the gulf between nationalist Ireland and unionist Ireland), strand three tackled a relationship that had been transformed by decades of co-existence as joint members of the international community: the Irish–British relationship. Notwithstanding the long-running, bitter struggle that had divided the two countries, important and exceptionally significant links had survived Irish independence in 1922, notably the common travel area (Ryan, 2001) and shared cultural experiences, such as the overspill of print and broadcast media from the UK to Ireland (Rafter, 2018, pp. 297–301). Joint British–Irish participation in the European integration process after 1973 added further depth to this, with the single market and the customs union reducing the visible significance of the border to little more than a symbolic one (Hayward & Murphy, 2018).

Like the North–South relationship, the East–West one was not traditionally supported by any kind of institutional links; such constitutional ties as survived after 1922 had virtually disappeared by 1936, and conclusively ended when Ireland's nominal connection with the Commonwealth expired in 1949. In the aftermath of the Anglo-Irish free trade agreement of 1965 relations improved further, though these came under strain with the outbreak of civil unrest in Northern Ireland in 1969. Nevertheless, an Irish–British Parliamentary Group bringing together members of the two parliaments flourished briefly in 1966–1969 (Coakley, 2017a, p. 200). A more enduring such body appeared at the end of the century. Agreed in principle at a British–Irish summit in 1981 and further encouraged by the Anglo-Irish agreement of 1985, the British–Irish Parliamentary Body finally came into existence in 1990. Initially comprising an equal number of British and Irish parliamentarians, after the Good Friday agreement its membership was expanded to include representatives of the UK's three devolved administrations (Scotland, Wales and Northern Ireland) and three crown dependencies (Jersey, Guernsey and the Isle of Man). As well as twice yearly plenary meetings that alternate between Ireland and the UK (of which 55 had taken place by October 2017), it has done a great deal of work in monitoring various aspects of the British–Irish relationship through four standing committees (British-Irish Parliamentary Assembly, 2018; Coakley, 2014, pp. 82–85).

Perhaps the most visible of the strand three institutions created by the Good Friday agreement was the British–Irish Council, a structure linking the governments of the eight jurisdictions represented in the British–Irish Parliamentary Assembly. As Walker (2001, p. 139) put it, the Council 'has gripped the imaginations of many people' and extravagant expectations regarding its capacity to transform relationships in these islands were expressed. But the reality of what the Council has delivered is more sober. It is, after all, as Bradley (2018) points out, consultative rather than executive in design. It may identify important cross-jurisdictional implications of public policy and offer policy advice, but governments are under little pressure to accept any of its recommendations. Nevertheless, it has been very active; 29 summit meeting had taken place by November 2017, with dozens of ministerial meetings within particular sectors. A formidable volume of useful reports on a wide range of specific areas has been compiled, offering at a minimum a useful information base on shared problems in these islands (British-Irish Council, 2018; Coakley, 2014, pp. 85–88).

The Good Friday agreement created an additional less visible institution, the British–Irish Intergovernmental Conference. This body amounted to a repackaging of the Anglo-Irish Intergovernmental Conference established by the Anglo-Irish agreement in 1985—an institution toxic to unionists as it gave the Irish government a formal voice in the internal affairs of Northern Ireland and a physical presence there through its joint secretariat at Maryfield, outside Belfast, staffed by British and Irish civil servants. The new body came into existence in December 1999, now excluded from involvement in areas where power was devolved to Stormont, but with a role in a range of important British–Irish policy domains, such as immigration, the common travel area and EU matters. Normally chaired by the Irish foreign minister and the Secretary of State for Northern Ireland, its membership extends to 'relevant' members of the Northern Ireland Executive (Coakley, 2014, pp. 79–82).

Unlike the strand two institutions, which have evolved little since they came into existence after 1998, the strand three institutions have mostly been further consolidated. The inter-parliamentary tier received a boost that was of at least nominal significance when it was redesignated an Assembly in 2008. The British–Irish Council was given more permanent status with the creation of a standing secretariat in Edinburgh in 2012. The Intergovernmental Conference, however, has in effect been allowed to lapse. The Good Friday agreement requires it to hold 'regular and frequent' meetings, but it has not met at ministerial level since February 2007, shortly before the restoration of devolved government in Northern Ireland. In 2012, the civil servants on the British side of its secretariat moved back to the Northern Ireland Office in Stormont. Though regular meetings between the British and Irish sides still take place, the latter now in effect functions as a diplomatic mission. Indeed, it is no longer mentioned in the section of the official web site that describes the main British–Irish institutions (Department of Foreign Affairs and Trade, 2018). Nevertheless, as the political vacuum in Northern Ireland continued, in late 2017 the Taoiseach began to contemplate reviving the British–Irish Intergovernmental Conference.[6]

This refocusing of the concerns of the two governments may be attributed in part to personnel turnover at the political level, with the disappearance of the Blair–Ahern partnership that had driven the peace process in its early years. The Cameron–Kenny alliance that succeeded this developed alternative channels of communication, as reflected in an agreement in 2012 to promote more institutionalised British–Irish cooperation at civil service level (Coakley, 2014, pp. 81–82). But the long-term trend has been towards lower priority for Northern Ireland at the most senior political level at a critical time, as Tannam (2018) concludes. This poses a singular challenge, in that, unlike Scotland and Wales, Northern Ireland lacks a voice at the Brexit negotiating table, and does not even have an agreed position on this (Hayward & Murphy, 2018).

The path of institutional development, of course, provides no more than a partial account of the evolution of the British–Irish relationship. The Good Friday agreement also marked a critical stage in the redefinition of this relationship, recording a historical detente between the Republic of Ireland and the UK. This reflected not just an increased willingness on the part of British governments to reach an accommodation with Irish nationalism, but a steady attenuation of the ambitions of Irish nationalism itself, and a much greater willingness on the part of its leaders to accept the constitutional status quo—whether explicitly or under the guise of traditional nationalist rhetoric (Coakley, 2017a, 2017b; Hayward, 2009). This was underwritten by obvious signs of collective British–Irish rapprochement, reflected in the first-ever state visit by a British monarch to independent Ireland, when Queen Elizabeth made a state visit in 2011, reciprocated in the first state visit of an Irish president to the UK by President Higgins in 2014.[7]

The more visible strand three institutions, then, the British–Irish Council and the British–Irish Parliamentary Assembly, were relatively uncontroversial, and appear to have acquired a stable existence. Notwithstanding their purely consultative role, they have helped to open new channels of communication between sovereign, devolved and crown dependent governments on these islands, and they have greatly widened the comparative policy information base. Indeed, they may come to have a particularly important role in the context of Brexit, since they are by now established forums for discussion of shared problems. At the same time, though, an important bilateral institution, the British–Irish Intergovernmental Conference, has been steadily receding in significance, in part because its mandate was greatly reduced while devolved government was up and running in Stormont. But it, too, may acquire a new importance in the context of Brexit.

Conclusion

On the morning after Good Friday, 1998, the *Irish Times* ran a front-page editorial that began memorably: 'Easter 1998: perhaps, in time, the date will resonate in the collective memory of our children and our grandchildren, just as 1916 or 1912 or 1689 or 1798 have done for those of earlier generations.' The newspaper went on to present the agreement as the start of a 'challenging experiment' whose object was to bring together 'the representatives of the people of all Ireland to agree how they might share this space of land upon which they have been cast by the tide of history' (*Irish Times*, 11 April 1998).

Twenty years later, it makes sense to ask whether the agreement has indeed delivered on its promise—the object of the articles in this collection. But it is doubtful whether, 20 years ago, anyone would have predicted that in answering this question we would also need to take account of the far-reaching implications of the UK's withdrawal from the EU. The Brexit question has indeed run through all of the articles in this collection. It is central in McCall's (2018) exploration of three major options for the design of borders in these islands in response to Brexit, where the units to be grouped behind a border with the outside might be either the entire British Isles, the existing UK, or the island of Great Britain. As Bradley's (2018) analysis of economic interdependence between North and South and between Ireland and Britain shows, redefinition of the North–South border will present a formidable challenge, made no easier by the very limited progress of strategic socio-economic policy-making in Northern Ireland. The centrality of Brexit is echoed by O'Leary (2018), Tannam (2018) and Hayward and Murphy (2018), with the latter reminding us that since joint British and Irish membership of the EU was central in the political accommodation in Northern Ireland, the undermining of this framework will have obvious consequences for this settlement—legal consequences, obviously, but also even more far-reaching political ones.

If we draw up a balance sheet relating to the three strands that have constituted the framework for this article, we end up with a mixed set of verdicts. First, domestic politics within Northern Ireland, though operating within what appeared to be the relatively robust framework of the Good Friday agreement, was derailed by events in late 2016 and early 2017. Prior to the collapse of the Executive, it looked as if the challenge of Brexit might actually promote joint action by the parties, notwithstanding their diverging positions on the EU. But the path towards 'normal' politics fell victim to growing inter-communal mistrust, spurred by the steady realignment of the nationalist–unionist socio-economic, political and demographic relationship. Second, systematic North–South political cooperation was kick-started by the Good Friday agreement, but the modest levels of institutionalised collaboration for which it made provision have been overshadowed by other forms of cooperation, driven by intergovernmental or EU-based pressures. In addition, the vigour of the North–South bodies has been compromised by their vulnerability to developments in strand one; the North–South political infrastructure can function as intended only when the institutions in Stormont are up and running. But developments at this level are particularly sensitive to the Brexit outcome, which, depending on its form, could either fatally undermine or greatly reinforce the all-island dimension. Third, this same dependence on the outcome of the EU–UK negotiations will have a major impact also on the British–Irish relationship. The ambitious architecture constructed by the Anglo-Irish agreement of 1985, as reshaped by the Good Friday agreement, has atrophied, leaving the Irish government with access either to direct (but not institutionalised) contact at governmental level or to multilateral discussion forums such as the British–Irish Council. Given potentially grave clashes of interest between the British and Irish sides, there is potential for deterioration in this relationship as the Brexit negotiations proceed.

Twenty years after its adoption, then, the Good Friday agreement continues to define the framework for the three sets of relationship it was designed to address. But its future will be substantially shaped by developments at European level, and in particular by the new relationship between the UK and the complex political entity it is currently trying to leave.

Notes

1. Projection based on the 2011 census by excluding the 2011 population aged 85 or more and adding new age groups based on the assumption that their composition would be the same as that of the 0–4 age cohort in 2011. This would generate an estimated Catholic population by community background in 2021 of 46.1%, with Protestants at 46.2% and others at 7.7%. In reality, the proportion of Catholics in this new group is likely to be higher than that estimated here since the new age cohorts are likely to have a higher proportion of Catholics than assumed here. 'Community background' refers to self-reported affiliation or, for those not so reporting, religion in which brought up.
2. Monitoring now includes private sector enterprises with more than 10 employees, but for consistency over time the data reported here refer only to enterprises with at least 26 employees.
3. Over the decade 2007–2016, the percentage of Catholics in the civil service fell on average 0.2% below the overall percentage in the monitored work force, while the percentage of Catholics in the private sector fell 0.4% below the overall percentage.

4. Petitions of concern requiring a cross-community vote may be triggered by 30 Assembly members. A cross-community vote, which may also arise for other reasons, requires support of a weighted majority (60%) of members present and voting, including at least 40% of each of the nationalist and unionist designations. In certain circumstances, 'parallel consent', a majority of unionist and nationalist members present and voting, may be required.
5. For example, one of the chief architects of the agreement, Bertie Ahern, is quoted as saying that 'a united Ireland could not be achieved by a simple majority poll in favour of constitutional change. ... Fifty percent plus one is not the way to do it. That would be a divisive thing to do' (*Belfast Telegraph*, 20 November 2008). Speaking in a BBC interview on 16 October 2017, Taoiseach Leo Varadkar said that a simple majority in a border poll would not be enough to secure a united Ireland, and that he did not favour changing Northern Ireland's constitutional position 'on a 50 per cent plus one basis' (*Irish News*, 18 October 2017).
6. For successive references by the Taoiseach to the prospective revival of the Conference, see *Dáil Debates Unrevised*, 961 (7), 21 November 2017 and 962 (1), 22 November 2017; *Irish Times*, 22 December 2017.
7. The very positive British interpretation of the significance of the visit was reflected in a glossy 88-page commemorative publication celebrating the visit (British Embassy, 2014).

References

Adams, G. (1998, March 12). A bridge to the future. *An Phoblacht*.

Arthur, P. (1974). *The people's democracy 1968–1973*. Belfast: Blackstaff.

Aunger, E. A. (1975). Religion and occupational class in Northern Ireland. *Economic and Social Review*, 7(1), 1–18.

Bradley, J. (2018). The Irish-Northern Irish economic relationship: The Belfast agreement, UK devolution and the EU. *Ethnopolitics*. doi:10.1080/17449057.2018.1472423

British Embassy. (2014). *Four days in April: A celebration of the inaugural state visit of President Michael D. Higgins to the United Kingdom in 2014*. Dublin: Harmonia, for the British Embassy.

British-Irish Council. (2018). *British-Irish Council*. Retrieved from www.britishirishcouncil.org/

British-Irish Parliamentary Assembly. (2018). *British-Irish Parliamentary Assembly*. Retrieved from www.britishirish.org/

Coakley, J. (2005). Northern Ireland and the British dimension. In J. Coakley & M. Gallagher (Eds.), *Politics in the Republic of Ireland* (4th ed., pp. 407–429). London: Routledge.

Coakley, J. (2014). British Irish institutional structures: Towards a new relationship. *Irish Political Studies*, 29(1), 76–97.

Coakley, J. (2016). Does Ulster still say no? Public opinion and the future of Northern Ireland. In J. A. Elkink & D. M. Farrell (Eds.), *The act of voting: Identities, institutions and locale* (pp. 35–55). London: Routledge.

Coakley, J. (2017a). Adjusting to partition: From irredentism to 'consent' in twentieth-century Ireland. *Irish Studies Review*, 25(2), 193–214.

Coakley, J. (2017b). Resolving international border disputes: The Irish experience. *Cooperation and Conflict*, 52 (3), 377–398.

Coakley, J. (2018a). Catholics in Northern Ireland: Changing political attitudes, 1968–2018. In P. Burgess (Ed.), *The contested identities of Ulster Catholics*. London: Palgrave Macmillan.

Coakley, J. (2018b). Northern Ireland and the British dimension. In J. Coakley & M. Gallagher (Eds.), *Politics in the Republic of Ireland* (6th ed., pp. 323–348). London: Routledge.

Coakley, J., & O'Dowd, L., (Eds.). (2007). *Crossing the border: New relationships between Northern Ireland and the Republic of Ireland*. Dublin: Irish Academic Press.

Department of Foreign Affairs and Trade. (2018). *The Good Friday agreement and today*. Retrieved from www.dfa.ie/our-role-policies/northern-ireland/the-good-friday-agreement-and-today/

Department of the Taoiseach. (2017). *All-Island civic dialogue: A compendium*. Dublin: Department of the Taoiseach and Department of Foreign Affairs and Trade.

Devlin, P. (1993). *Straight left: An autobiography*. Belfast: Blackstaff.

Doyle, J. (2010). The politics of the transformation of policing. In J. Doyle (Ed.), *Policing the narrow ground* (pp. 167–211). Dublin: Royal Irish Academy.

Doyle, J., & Connolly, E. (2017). *Brexit and the future of Northern Ireland* (Working Paper no. 1-2017). Dublin: Brexit Institute, Dublin City University.

Equality Commission for Northern Ireland. (2002–2017). *Monitoring report no.12 [no. 13, 14, … 27]: A profile of the Northern Ireland workforce*. Belfast: Equality Commission for Northern Ireland.

EU Commission. (2017, December 8). *Joint report from the negotiators of the European Union and the United Kingdom Government on progress during phase 1 of negotiations under Article 50 TEU on the United Kingdom's orderly withdrawal from the European Union*. TF50 (2017) 19 – Commission to EU 27. Retrieved from ec.europa.eu/commission/publications/j

Executive Office. (2018). *Labour force survey religion report 2016: Annual update – January 2018*. Belfast: Northern Ireland Statistics and Research Agency.

Foster, A., & McGuinness, M. (2016). *Letter to the Prime Minister, 10 August*. Belfast: Executive Office. Retrieved from www.executiveoffice-ni.gov.uk/publications/letter-prime-minister-rt-hon-theresa-may-mp

Gaffney, F., Deane, J. P., & Ó Gallachóir, B. P. (2017). A 100 year review of electricity policy in Ireland (1916–2016). *Energy Policy, 105*, 67–79.

Hayes, B. C., & McAllister, I. (2013). *Conflict to peace: Politics and society in Northern Ireland over half a century*. Manchester: Manchester University Press.

Hayward, K. (2009). *Irish nationalism and European integration: The official redefinition of the Island of Ireland*. Manchester: Manchester University Press.

Hayward, K., & Murphy, M. C. (2018). The EU's influence on the peace process and agreement in Northern Ireland in light of Brexit. *Ethnopolitics*. doi:10.1080/17449057.2018.1472426

Hayward, K., & Phinnemore, D. (2018). *The Northern Ireland/Ireland border, regulatory alignment and Brexit: Principles and options in light of the UK-EU joint report of 8 December 2017* (Briefing Paper 3). Belfast: Queen's University Brexit Briefing Series.

Howard, K. (2007). Civil society: The permeability of the North-South border. In J. Coakley & L. O'Dowd (Eds.), *Crossing the border: New relationships between Northern Ireland and the Republic of Ireland* (pp. 87–103). Dublin: Irish Academic Press.

Independent Commission on Policing for Northern Ireland. (1999). *A new beginning: Policing in Northern Ireland: The report of the Independent Commission on Policing for Northern Ireland* (Patten Report). Belfast: HMSO.

Lagana, G. (2017). A preliminary investigation on the genesis of EU cross-border cooperation on the island of Ireland. *Space and Polity, 21*(3), 289–302.

Lynn, B. (1997). *Holding the ground: The nationalist party in Northern Ireland, 1945–72*. Aldershot: Ashgate.

Matthews, N., & Pow, J. (2017). A fresh start? The Northern Ireland Assembly election 2016. *Irish Political Studies, 32*(2), 311–326.

McCall, C. (2018). Brexit, bordering and people on the island of Ireland. *Ethnopolitics*. doi:10.1080/17449057.2018.1472425

McCluskey, C. (1989). *Up off their knees: A commentary on the civil rights movement in Northern Ireland*. Ireland: Conn McCluskey and Associates.

McQuaid, R., & Hollywood, E. (2008). *Educational migration and non-return in Northern Ireland: A report prepared for the Equality Commission for Northern Ireland*. Belfast: Equality Commission for Northern Ireland.

Mulcahy, A. (2006). *Policing Northern Ireland: Conflict, legitimacy and reform*. Cullompton: Willan.

Murphy, M. C. (2014). *Northern Ireland and the European Union: The dynamics of a changing relationship*. Manchester: Manchester University Press.

Nolan, P. (2012). *Northern Ireland peace monitoring report number one*. Belfast: Community Relations Council.

Nolan, P. (2013). *Northern Ireland peace monitoring report number two*. Belfast: Community Relations Council.

Nolan, P. (2014). *Northern Ireland peace monitoring report number three*. Belfast: Community Relations Council.

Northern Ireland Office. (2010). *Police (Northern Ireland) Act 2000 – review of temporary recruitment provisions: Consultation paper*. London: Northern Ireland Office.

Northern Ireland Statistics and Research Agency. (2018). *Census 2011*. Retrieved from www.nisra.gov.uk/statistics/census/2011-census

O'Leary, B. (2018). The twilight of the United Kingdom and Tiocaidh ár lá: Twenty years after the Good Friday agreement. *Ethnopolitics*. doi:10.1080/17449057.2018.1473114

O'Leary, B., & McGarry, J. (1996). *The politics of antagonism: Understanding Northern Ireland* (2nd ed.). London: Athlone Press.

Osborne, R. D., & Shuttleworth, I. (2004). Fair employment in Northern Ireland. In R. D. Osborne & I. Shuttleworth (Eds.), *Fair employment in Northern Ireland: A generation on* (pp. 1–23). Belfast: Blackstaff.

Phinnemore, D., & Hayward, K. (2017). *UK withdrawal ('Brexit') and the Good Friday agreement [PE 596.826]*. Brussels: European Parliament Policy Department for Citizens' Rights and Constitutional Affairs.

Police Service of Northern Ireland. (2018a). *Security situation statistics*. Retrieved from www.psni.police.uk/inside-psni/Statistics/security-situation-statistics/

Police Service of Northern Ireland. (2018b). *Workforce composition statistics*. Retrieved from www.psni.police.uk/inside-psni/Statistics/workforce-composition-statistics/

Pollak, A. (2017). Northern intransigeance and southern indifference: North-South cooperation since the Belfast agreement. In N. Ó Dochartaigh, K. Hayward, & E. Meehan (Eds.), *Dynamics of political chance in Ireland: Making and breaking a divided Island* (pp. 178–192). London: Routledge.

Purdie, B. (1990). *Politics in the streets: The origins of the civil rights movement in Northern Ireland*. Belfast: Blackstaff.

Rafter, K. (2018). The media and politics. In J. Coakley & M. Gallagher (Eds.), *Politics in the Republic of Ireland* (6th ed., pp. 295–319). London: Routledge.

Ruane, J., & Todd, J. (1996). *The dynamics of conflict in Northern Ireland: Power, conflict and emancipation*. Cambridge: Cambridge University Press.

Ruane, J., & Todd, J. (2014). History, structure and action in the settlement of complex conflicts: The Northern Ireland case. *Irish Political Studies*, *29*(1), 15–36.

Russell, R. (2004). Employment profiles of Protestants and Catholics: A decade of monitoring. In R. D. Osborne & I. Shuttleworth (Eds.), *Fair employment in Northern Ireland: A generation on* (pp. 24–48). Belfast: Blackstaff.

Ryan, B. (2001). The common travel area between Britain and Ireland. *Modern Law Review*, *64*(6), 831–854.

Schubotz, D. (2008). Is there a Protestant brain drain from Northern Ireland? *Shared Space: A Research Journal on Peace, Conflict and Community Relations in Northern Ireland*, *6*, 5–19.

Soares, A. (2016). Living within and outside unions: The consequences of Brexit for Northern Ireland. *Journal of Contemporary European Research*, *12*(4), 835–843.

Staunton, E. (2001). *The nationalists of Northern Ireland, 1918–1973*. Dublin: Columba Press.

Stevenson, J. (2017). Does Brexit threaten peace in Northern Ireland? *Survival*, *59*(3), 111–128.

Tannam, E. (1999). *Cross-border cooperation in the Republic of Ireland and Northern Ireland*. Basingstoke: Macmillan.

Tannam, E. (2018). Intergovernmental and cross-border civil service cooperation: The Good Friday agreement and Brexit. *Ethnopolitics*. doi:10.1080/17449057.2018.1472422

Todd, J. (2014). Thresholds of state change: Changing British state institutions and practices in Northern Ireland after direct rule. *Political Studies*, *62*(3), 522–538.

Todd, J. (2017). The effectiveness of the agreement: International conditions and contexts. In N. Ó Dochartaigh, K. Hayward, & E. Meehan (Eds.), *Dynamics of political chance in Ireland: Making and breaking a divided Island* (pp. 61–74). London: Routledge.

Tonge, J. (2002). *Northern Ireland: Conflict and change* (2nd ed.). Harlow: Pearson Longman.

Tonge, J. (2017). *The impact and consequences of Brexit for Northern Ireland* [European Parliament Briefing, Constitutional Affairs, PE 583 116]. Retrieved from www.europarl.europa.eu/

Walker, G. (2001). The British–Irish Council. In R. Wilford (Ed.), *Aspects of the Belfast agreement* (pp. 129–141). Oxford: Oxford University Press.

Wilson, R. (2016). *Northern Ireland peace monitoring report number four*. Belfast: Community Relations Council.

Postscript: New British Questions or *2019 And All That!*

BRENDAN O'LEARY

William Caruthers Sellars and Robert Yeatman famously satirized the teaching of the history of England in 1930. A fresh version of their work is long overdue, perhaps with the provisional title *2019 And All That! A Memorable History of the UK's Attempted Departure from the EU Comprising, All the Parts You Can Remember Including Two Hundred and Eight Roads in Ireland, Over One Hundred and Forty Economic Functions, Three Bad Prime Ministers who fell out with Europe, and Two Genuine Dates.* One of those dates is 29 March 2019, when the UK is officially scheduled to leave the EU. Another is December 2017, when this special issue was being closed. At that juncture, the EU-27 and UK negotiators reached a progress agreement on 'the UK's orderly withdrawal from the EU' (The European Union and United Kingdom Government, 2017). Of its 96 paragraphs, 14 were devoted to 'the unique circumstances' of Northern Ireland, and the negotiators solemnly affirmed they would protect the Belfast/Good Friday Agreement 'in all its parts,' and pledged they would work to ensure 'the avoidance of a hard border' (2017, para 43).[1] Following up, on 19 March 2018 a 129-page draft agreement on the UK's withdrawal was published, including a draft protocol on Northern Ireland, widely known as the 'back-stop' solution.

The back-stop is to be executed if no other satisfactory means exists of maintaining as frictionless a border as possible between Ireland and the UK. A full legal chapter has been published that would establish a common regulatory area regarding Northern Ireland, to be administered by the EU and the UK. Northern Ireland would remain in the EU's customs unions and apply EU law regarding internal taxation, non-tariff barriers to trade, VAT and excise duties, and agriculture and fisheries; the island would have a single electricity market; environmental regulation of exports and imports from and to Northern Ireland would operate under EU law (European Union and United Kingdom Government, 2018, Protocol, Ch. III, Articles 3–7); and the EU's Court of Justice would have final jurisdiction over all these functions (European Union and United Kingdom

Government, 2018, Article 11). The entirety of the March 19 text represents the EU's position, including its draft statutory language; the UK, by contrast, has so far only agreed to some of its provisions.

Prudence has long suggested that the UK authorities would want to avoid the creation of opportunities for dissident Irish republicans to reignite conflict through closing 208 roads (Hutton, 2018), erecting fortified barriers on a newly restricted land-border, or re-establishing pillar boxes manned by armed soldiers. But, after any meaningful UKEXIT there has to be a border—or more than one border—between the UK and the EU. A customs border if the UK leaves the EU customs union; a regulatory border if the UK leaves the single market; and a security border if current cooperation fails (including a border restraining freedom of movement if the Common Travel Area between the UK and Ireland cannot be sustained).

The key questions are where the border(s) should be, and how they are to be administered. On the island of Ireland, following the partition delimitation that separates 5 of Northern Ireland's 6 counties from 4 of sovereign Ireland's 26? Or at ports and airports in Great Britain (and in both parts of Ireland), which would make the Irish Sea an administrative border? Regarding Ireland's European border with the UK, the Commission, Council, Parliament, and the Court of Justice of the European Union have standing, including over how border-related functions can be performed (some of them may take place away from the demarcated border). To clarify the cross-border cooperation obligated under the Good Friday Agreement a mapping exercise has been conducted by officials, 'which shows that North-South cooperation relies to a significant extent on a common European Union legal and policy framework' (2017, para 47). Over 140 functions or economic activities have been identified as linked to North–South cooperation. 'In the absence of agreed solutions' [to border questions and compliance with the 1998 Agreement] the UK has pledged (2017, para 49) to maintain full alignment 'with those rules of the Internal Market and the Customs Union which, now *or in the future* support North-South cooperation, the all-island economy and the protection of the 1998 Agreement' (author's emphasis). Whether this commitment is confined to the aforementioned 140 activities or covers the full scope of the Internal Market and the Customs Union remains to be determined, but a single regulatory regime will operate on the island for all cross-border functions deemed necessary under the 1998 Agreement.[2] Having no border for 140+ functions, but having border(s) for others scarcely guarantees frictionless border(s).

Over time, three Conservative UK Prime Ministers—Margaret Thatcher, David Cameron, and Theresa May—have so mishandled the UK's membership of the EU that to date 26 member-states of the EU are aligned in solidarity with Ireland's positions on the UK's prospective exit, and its consequences for the Good Friday Agreement. Two matters, however, are agreed between the EU-27 and the UK, and seem unlikely to change. *As and when* the UK leaves the EU, Northern Ireland will have one unique status, namely its provisions for citizenship. Those born in Northern Ireland, as per the 1998 Agreement and Ireland's modified constitution, will continue to be entitled to both Irish and UK citizenship—and through their Irish citizenship rights will continue to be entitled to EU citizenship.[3] No one born in Northern Ireland stands to lose their EU citizenship and mobility rights, but they may well be placed in the curious position of losing their right to vote for MEPs in the European Parliament, a subject that may wend its way to the Court of Justice of the European Union.[4] The parties have also pledged themselves to 'examine arrangements required to give effect to the ongoing exercise of, and access to, their EU rights, opportunities and benefits' (European Union and United Kingdom

Government, 2017, para 52).[5] Second, *if and when* Northern Ireland's votes to reunify with Ireland, then Northern Ireland would automatically become part of the EU. There had scarcely been any doubt on the question, given the precedent of German reunification, but those who feared the prospect of a Spanish or other member-state veto, have had that fear removed. These clarifications matter. The Northern Irish (unlike the Great British) retain EU citizenship, and those keen on staying within the EU, or returning to it, or who are adversely affected by UKEXIT, have incentives to vote for Irish reunification.

In December 2017, both parties pledged to respect the constitutional status of Northern Ireland, and the principle of consent, to please unionists (namely, it remains part of the UK as long as a majority so wishes), with the UK government fully supporting 'Northern Ireland's position as an integral part of the United Kingdom' (so far as that is consistent with the 1998 Agreement) (2017, para 44).[6] Two crucial paragraphs followed, however, largely but not exclusively dealing with UK-Ireland relations:

45. The United Kingdom respects Ireland's ongoing membership of the European Union and all of the corresponding rights and obligations that entails, in particular Ireland's place in the Internal Market and the Customs Union. The United Kingdom also recalls its commitment to preserving the integrity of its internal market and Northern Ireland's place within it, as the United Kingdom leaves the European Union's Internal Market and Customs Union.

46. The commitments and principles outlined in this joint report will not pre-determine the outcome of wider discussions on the future relationship between the European Union and the United Kingdom, and are, as necessary, specific to the unique circumstances on the island of Ireland. *They are made and must be upheld in all circumstances, irrespective of the nature of any future agreement between the European Union and the United Kingdom.* (Author's emphasis)

Since a customs union requires a common border and external tariff for all its members, and because the EU's Single Market requires a common external regulatory border, it follows that the UK has pledged to remain in the equivalent of the customs union and the single market (at least regarding Northern Ireland) if that is necessary to avoid a hard border; otherwise, its pledges are meaningless. An understatement in paragraph 47 defines the scope of the problem: 'the United Kingdom's departure from the European Union gives rise to substantial challenges to the maintenance and development of North-South cooperation.' But, responding to these challenges, and reiterating all its other commitments, including to North–South co-operation, and to its 'guarantee of avoiding a hard border,' the UK has indicated that it would seek to meet all these goals through the [new] EU-UK relationship, but,

Should this not be possible: The United Kingdom will propose specific solutions to address the unique circumstances of the island of Ireland. *In the absence of agreed solutions*, the United Kingdom *will maintain full alignment with those rules of the Internal Market and the Customs Union which, now or in the future, support North-South cooperation, the all-island economy and the protection of the 1998 Agreement.* (2017, para 49, author's emphasis)

On the face of this text, and absent miraculous technological breakthroughs that obviate the need for any border, or some special bespoke partnership between the UK and the EU-27 which the European Commission and Council have so far steadily refused, and for which negotiating time is running out, the UK is obliged either to stay in its entirety within the EU customs union and single market *or* it is committed to allowing Northern Ireland to do so, i.e. to permitting a differentiated UKEXIT, to which Mrs May had once been adamantly opposed. There is no third way known to those currently alive, especially to those capable of reading texts accurately. Having radically narrowed its options, the UK government immediately offloaded its responsibilities, handing the DUP and Sinn Féin a future opportunity to cooperate, or to exercise a veto. It promised that, 'in the absence of agreed solutions, [it] will ensure that no regulatory barriers' develop between Northern Ireland and Great Britain, 'unless, consistent with the 1998 Agreement, the Northern Ireland Executive and Assembly agree that distinct arrangements are appropriate for Northern Ireland.' So, on face of the text, it is up to Northern Ireland whether it opts for special arrangements.[7] To exercise these rights it would naturally be helpful if the Northern Executive and Assembly were restored, but currently the DUP which supports the minority Conservative government blocks that possibility.

The EU-27 and the UK have agreed that they will 'establish mechanisms to ensure the implementation and oversight of any specific arrangement to safeguard the integrity of the EU Internal Market and the Customs Union' (2017, para 51). That queues for resolution the question of what court or courts will perform such safeguarding, and what role(s) they might perform regarding the draft protocol of March 2018. The UK has also committed itself to recognize Ireland's rights and duties within the EU, which therefore commits it to respect Ireland's ability to respect the EU's four freedoms, including freedom of movement of persons. The UK has also, impliedly, bound itself not to adopt any laws or policies that would require the EU to impose border controls (Bruton, 2017).[8]

The December progress agreement stated that the Common Travel Area between the UK and Ireland will continue to be respected by the EU; and that the UK 'confirms and accepts that Common Travel Area and associated rights and privileges can continue to operate without affecting Ireland's obligations under Union law, in particular with respect to free movement for EU citizens;' while the EU, the UK and Ireland will fully respect 'the rights of natural persons conferred by Union law.'[9] Equivalent provisions, fully agreed, are in the subsequent draft protocol (2018, Chapter II Article 2). The Conservatives, however, are publicly pledged to end freedom of movement from the EU. How exactly will that be compatible with the preservation of the Common Travel Area in its current form? Namely, how will an EU citizen, not from Ireland, who has lawfully traveled to Ireland, be prevented from entering the UK through Northern Ireland? We await guidance. Three answers present themselves: non-border-based employment and residency checks in the UK; the agreement of identity cards within the Common Travel Area; or, the UK quietly allows Ireland to become a back door illegal migration channel. Further answers there will have to be.

The conditioning of the UK's withdrawal agreement with the EU-27, as regards Ireland, is not confined to questions related to the border, agriculture, the regulation of capital, commerce, and energy, or the common travel area. The UK has also committed 'to *ensuring* that no diminution of rights is caused by its departure from the European Union' including protection against forms of discrimination that are enshrined in EU law. 'The United Kingdom commits to *facilitating* the related work of the institutions and bodies, established by the 1998 Agreement, in upholding human rights and equality standards' (The European Union and United Kingdom Government, 2017, para 53, author's emphasis). The first of these commitments is strong, and presumably requires either direct acceptance of the jurisdiction of the Court of Justice of the European Union, or, indirect acceptance of the same, through a court which effectively provides the equivalent, for example, the EFTA court.[10] The European Commission had already emphasized that 'the Good Friday Agreement requires equivalent standards of protection of rights in Ireland and Northern Ireland' (2017, p. 4). The question now becomes what dispute resolution and enforcement mechanism can maintain that obligation. The second commitment, merely to facilitation, is obviously weaker, but the Northern Ireland Human Rights and Equality Commissions established under the Good Friday Agreement are likely safe from abolition or resource-starvation.[11] These judgments are partly confirmed by the draft Protocol of March 2018, in which the UK pledges to ensure

> no diminution of rights, safeguards and equality of opportunity as set out in the 1998 Agreement ... including in the area of protection against discrimination as enshrined in the provisions of Union law' which will be listed in a detailed Annex in due course ...

The politics behind the text of the progress agreement was as interesting as the text. The UK government had surrendered to the EU-27 on all preconditions for passage to the next phase of the negotiations—i.e. it pledged to pay its exit bill, accept all EU laws and Court rulings during the proposed standstill transition, to accept the protection of EU citizen rights placed in jeopardy by its departure, and has made specific commitments regarding the border and the 1998 Agreement—in all its parts. May was, however, forced to leave Brussels as she was about to sign the text, and return to bargain with the DUP for a week. Arlene Foster's party was unhappy because the original text emphatically implied that Northern Ireland would be treated differently to the UK.[12]

First Minister Foster, with her colleagues arrayed behind her, declared on the internal Stormont staircase that Northern Ireland must leave the EU on exactly the same basis as the UK as a whole. The Conservatives and the DUP had not successfully communicated, or someone had been left in the dark. Had May misled Foster, or had Foster (and her deputy Dodds) faced a rebellion within the DUP? Had there been plans to put the Ulster unionists under the Brexit bus? It was unavoidably clear that 'A British government at an international summit was humiliated by a minority party pursuing a minority point of view.'[13] To pacify the DUP, and to secure the Scottish Tories, worried about reach-across implications for Scotland, May agreed to modify the progress agreement. Overlooked by the Irish government and the DUP, and with calls offstage from the Scottish Parliament, Welsh Assembly and the London Mayor, changes were made to the text, in which May put the whole of the UK on the hook for a soft exit. In committing to mirror the customs union and the European single market's regulations as regards the North she may have committed the entire UK to the functional equivalent of being in both.[14]

The sole way to achieve a frictionless border across Ireland after the UK leaves the EU—which the DUP and Conservatives say they want—and to treat Northern Ireland no differently from Great Britain—ditto—was to sign up to UKEXITINO, a UK exit in name only. May had conceded what she had said she would not concede, special status for Northern Ireland. Then, under pressure from Foster's DUP, she had partially reversed herself, but at the expense of getting into the second phase of the negotiations with almost all her leverage gone. Differently put, the DUP may have temporarily blocked Northern Ireland from having 'special status,' but at the price of a queer 'special status' for the UK as a whole—within the UK, Northern Ireland has the special status of determining whether Great Britain can diverge from EU customs and regulations more than Northern Ireland. We shall see whether this text, a humiliation for the London government, can hold. Nothing is agreed until everything is agreed, but definitive decisions cannot long be deferred.

Unionists have been assured that Northern Ireland will not be treated differently than the rest of the UK *unless* the Northern Executive and Assembly decide otherwise—a moot point given their current non-functioning. There plainly remains here an opening to a differentiated UKEXIT from the EU. The draft legal text of the Protocol, which is not fully agreed by the UK, makes that emphatically clear. The onus remains on the UK, within months, to provide technological or other resolutions which obviate the need for a hard border. None, however, are known to exist, except in the future perfect tense or in the mind of Boris Johnson, the UK Foreign Secretary. Article 15 of the draft Protocol of March 2018, provides that:

> Should a subsequent agreement between the Union and United Kingdom which addresses the unique circumstances on the island of Ireland, avoids a hard border and protects the 1998 Agreement in all its dimensions, become applicable after the entry into force of the Withdrawal Agreement, this Protocol shall not apply, or shall cease to apply, in whole or in part, from the date of application of such subsequent agreement and in accordance with that agreement.

What this provision does not say is that any future EU-27 and UK agreement would almost certainly become a 'mixed' treaty, i.e. it would affect matters other than trade, and would therefore likely require unanimous consent among the EU-27, grant Ireland a veto, and quite possibly require an affirmative vote from Ireland's public in a constitutional referendum.

The text of the March 2018 draft Withdrawal Agreement was color-coded. *Green* marks full agreement; *yellow* marks agreement in principle, subject to drafting considerations; and the parts without any color-highlighting (*white*) remain to be negotiated. It is purely coincidental that this color-scheme resembles the Irish tricolor of green, white, and orange. The text of the Protocol is in white but paragraph 49 of the December agreement was agreed by the UK: the 'back-stop.' Unless the UK reneges from the position it took to advance the negotiations, and unless it is allowed to renege from this provision by the EU-27, this provision has to be part of the withdrawal agreement, or else there will be no exit agreement—and a cliff-face or hard UKEXIT.

Barring that possibility, as this issue goes to press the default outcome for now is that Northern Ireland will remain substantively inside the EU's regulatory structures. How that resolution fits with Great Britain is most easily resolved by the rest of the UK staying within the single market and the customs union, but that will trigger tension among the self-styled Brexiteers, who have described such status, as that of a vassal state (though such status is self-chosen). A break between the Conservative government and the DUP is also possible, but its contours cannot currently be foreseen. A London government, keen to complete a withdrawal settlement with the EU-27, one which gives it policy freedom to make trade deals with third countries, may well pressurize Northern Ireland (read the DUP) in 2018–2019 to show flexibility regarding North–South relations, and allow for the possibility of genuine regulatory and customs barriers in the Irish Sea to give Great Britain greater flexibility. One can imagine funding regimes to support that goal that might make such a differentiated UKEXIT at least temporarily palatable to some within the DUP. But if that path is not trodden an historical irony may materialize. Nearly a 100 years after the treaty that obliged the Irish Free State to stay within the British empire and rejected republican status for Ireland, the treaty encompassing the UK's withdrawal from the EU will be conditioned by Great Britain's obligations to preserve the Good Friday Agreement in all its parts, at the behest of Ireland and the EU-27. Differently put, 'London is effectively a prisoner of Belfast,' and 'Britain can have any Brexit it likes, so long as it is green' (O'Toole, 2017b). *1066 and All That* suggested that whenever the English sought to solve the Irish question, for example, by the use of the sword or by 'blood-Orangemen,' the Irish would change the question. Resolving UKExit questions, all now understand, means that Northern Ireland changes the subject. As the price of its divorce from the EU must Great Britain leave Northern Ireland more within the guardianship of the EU than the rest of the UK? If it is loyal to Northern Ireland's loyalists must it surrender the entire UK into the guardianship of the Customs Union and Single Market? Differently put, for Great Britain to be free must Northern Ireland be partially surrendered to the EU?

Notes

1. The Agreement 'must be protected in all its parts,' extending 'to the practical application of the 1998 Agreement on the island of Ireland and to the totality of the relationships set out in the Agreement' (2017, para 42). The UK specifically recalled its commitment to protecting the Agreement's operation, 'including its subsequent implementation agreements, and to the effective operation of each of the institutions and bodies under them,' and 'to the avoidance of a hard border, including any physical infrastructure of related checks and controls' (2017, para 43).

2. The 1998 Agreement specified twelve areas for co-operation and implementation: agriculture, aquaculture and marine matters, education, environment, health, inland fisheries, relevant EU programs, social security/social welfare, tourism, transport, urban and rural development, and waterways. Cooperation is not, however, confined to these subjects: there is an all-island energy, including electricity, market. For the view/hope that little regulatory convergence would be required to square 'Northern Ireland's Brexit circle' see Emerson (2017).

   The commitment to the maintenance of a common regulatory regimes cannot be confined to the 12 sectors, however, because 'the all-island economy' is also referenced, and the reference to 'in the future' is open-ended: legally, every future change in EU law, regulations, and directives, will have to be applied in both parts of Ireland.

3. Turkish Cypriots currently may obtain Cypriot, and thereby EU passports, but the European *acquis communautaire* does not extend to the so-called Republic of Northern Cyprus.

4. Whether Ireland could arrange, with EU consent, for one or more MEPs to be elected from among its citizens living in Northern Ireland is not something I have sought to explore.

5. The recital to the draft Protocol recognizes the EU Union citizenship of Irish citizens in Northern Ireland and references the British-Irish treaty of 1999, The European Union and The Government of the United Kingdom of Great Britain and Northern Ireland (2018, p. 109).

6. Unlike UK governments the DUP has never endorsed the 1998 Agreement, unconvincingly claiming that the Saint Andrews Agreement was a completely different agreement—to which they reluctantly acceded.

7. An addendum, in the same paragraph, declared that, 'In all circumstances,' the UK 'will continue to ensure the same unfettered access for Northern Ireland's businesses to the whole of the United Kingdom internal market' (2017, para 50).

8. Chapter II, Article 2 of the draft Protocol, which is agreed, obligates the UK to ensure that the Common Travel Area 'without affecting the obligations of Ireland under [EU] Union law,' The European Union and The Government of the United Kingdom of Great Britain and Northern Ireland (2018, p. 110).

9. European Union and United Kingdom Government (2017, para 54). What is at stake here is whether, as seems likely, the EU has agreed that British citizens may have more favorable treatment in Ireland than EU citizens (Maher, 2017).

10. 'The European Economic Area (EEA) unites the EU Member States and the three EEA EFTA States (Iceland, Liechtenstein, and Norway) into an Internal Market governed by the same basic rules. These rules aim to enable goods, services, capital, and persons to move freely about the EEA in an open and competitive environment, a concept referred to as the four freedoms,' http://www.efta.int/eea. In a policy paper published in August 2017, looking forward to a future enforcement and dispute resolution mechanism with the EU, the UK's Department for Exiting the European Union signaled its wish to end the *direct* jurisdiction of the Court of Justice of the European Union, leaving open the possibility of the EFTA Court enforcing such an agreement, a court widely acknowledged to defer to the CJEU (on its jurisprudence see Fredriksen, 2015; HM Government, 2017a).

11. The attendant complexities for the protection of rights have been treated well elsewhere (McCrudden, 2017a, 2017b).

12. Earlier in the second week of November 2017, a paper was leaked that had circulated among EU ambassadors. It stated that the sole means to avoid a hard border across Ireland was for Northern Ireland to remain in the customs union and the single market, or the functional equivalent thereof; the customs and regulatory border between the UK and the EU would therefore have to be in the Irish Sea. Amid outraged reactions from the DUP and Conservative MPs, *The Sun* newspaper suggested that Sinn Féin/IRA (sic!) was leaning on the Irish government. The leaked paper helped oblige the UK to come up with express text on how it was going to address the border question, moving beyond 'magical thinking,' as Barnier had called the UK's paper of August (HM Government, 2017b); see the informed discussion in Connelly (2017). For the EU and the DUP to protect the 1998 Agreement in all its parts, North–South cooperation, and the all-island economy, there can be no regulatory divergence from the customs union and the single market. *QED.* Since the EU was in the driving seat, it obliged the UK to choose between no divergence for Northern Ireland and no divergence for the UK as a whole. The final text of the progress agreement, discussed above, implies that the UK has opted for no divergence for the UK as a whole, while enabling Northern Ireland to opt for regulatory convergence on its own.

13. Jenkins (2017): the DUP received less than 1% of the votes in the UK as a whole. A similar judgment was the estimation that the DUP has alienated a swathe of British opinion that would now prefer to see the DUP as a foreign body in its body politic (O'Toole, 2017a).

14. 'It is now far more likely that Britain will stay in the customs union and the single market. It is also more likely that Brexit will not in fact happen' (O'Toole, 2017b).

References

Bruton, J. (2017, December 29). Border pledge has complicated Brexit. *Irish Times.*

Carruthers Sellar, W., & Yeatman, R. J. (1930). *1066 and all that. A memorable history of England comprising, all the parts you can remember including one hundred and one good things, five bad kings, and two genuine dates* (7th ed.). London: Methuen.

Connelly, T. (2017, November 19). The Brexit veto: How and why Ireland raised the stakes. *RTE.ie.*

Emerson, N. (2017, December 7). Brexit border row is another little DUP victory on road to defeat. *Irish Times.*

Fredriksen, H. H. (2015). The EEA and the case law of the CJEU: Incorporation without participation? In E. O. Eriksen & J. E. Fossum (Eds.), *The European Union's non-members: Independence under hegemony?* (pp. 102–117). London: Routledge.

HM Government. (2017a). *Enforcement and dispute resolution – a future partnership paper.* London. Retrieved from https://www.gov.uk/government/uploads/system/uploads/attachment_data/file/639609/Enforcement_ and_dispute_resolution.pdf

HM Government. (2017b). *Northern Ireland and Ireland: Position paper.* London: Northern Ireland Office & Department for Exiting the European Union.

Hutton, B. (2018, April 26). Ireland has 208 border crossings, officials from north and south agree. *Irish Times.*

Jenkins, S. (2017, December 5). Theresa May must call the DUP's bluff – this EU deal has to happen. *The Guardian.*

Maher, I. (2017, October). The common travel area: More than just travel. *A Royal Irish Academy – British Academy Brexit Briefing.*

McCrudden, C. (2017a). *An early deal-breaker? EU citizens' rights in the UK after Brexit, and the future role of the European court of justice.* Retrieved from http://ukconstitutionallaw.org

McCrudden, C. (2017b, October). The Good Friday Agreement, Brexit, and rights. *A Royal Irish Academy – British Academy Brexit Briefing.*

O'Toole, F. (2017a, September 28). Brexit's Irish question. *New York Review of Books*.

O'Toole, F. (2017b, December 8). Ireland has just saved the UK from the madness of a hard Brexit. *Irish Times*.

The European Union, & The Government of the United Kingdom of Great Britain and Northern Ireland. (2018). *Draft agreement on the withdrawal of the United Kingdom of Great Britain and Northern Ireland from the European Union and the European Atomic Energy Community.* Highlighting the progress made (coloured version) in the negotiation round with the UK of 16–19 March 2018. (European Commission, ed.). Brussels.

The European Union, & the United Kingdom Government. (2017). *Joint report from the negotiators of the European Union and the United Kingdom Government: On progress during phase 1 of negotiations under article 50 TEU on the United Kingdom's orderly withdrawal from the European Union* (pp. 1–15). (European Commission, ed.). Brussels.

Index

Adams, G. 8, 92–3
Ahern, B. 26
The Anglo-Irish Agreement 23
Aunger, E. A. 88

Balance of Competences Review 59
Barnier, Michel 54–5
Blair, Tony 26, 27
Bradley, J. 4, 87, 93, 97–9
Brady, Hugo 79
Brexit: cross-border economic cooperation and
    50–1; and intergovernmental and civil service
    cooperation 31–6; Northern Ireland and 63–6
Brexit bordering 72–4; Britain 76–9; isles of
    Britain and Ireland 79–80; United Kingdom
    75–6
British-Irish Intergovernmental Conference
    (B-IGC) 10, 24–5, 27
British–Irish intergovernmental cooperation and
    EU 56–7
British–Irish relationship: nationalism and
    unionism 85–93; normalisation of 96–8; North
    and South 93–6

Cameron, David 27, 32, 60, 78, 104
civil service cross-border cooperation, Brexit on
    35–6
Coakley, John 4
Colvin, C. 62
Coveney, Simon 34, 54
cross-border cooperation: and Brexit 50–1; and
    East–West economic relationships 42–4;
    economic development in 46–7
cross-border trade 47–50

Davis, David 34
The Democratic Unionist Party (DUP) 4–9,
    12–13, 26
Department for Exiting the EU (DexEU) 35–6
The Department of Foreign Affairs 35
The Department of the Taoiseachs
    International 35
d'Hondt allocation rule 2, 4, 6, 9

Dicey, A. V. 11
Dodds, Nigel 9–10
The Downing Street Declaration 7

East–West cooperation and Belfast Agreement 44
Eastwood, Colum 8
economic policy making 48–50
European Economic Community (EEC) 55–6
Europeanisation 71–2
European Parliament (EP) 56–7
European Policy Coordination Unit (EPCU) 58
European Union (EU): and cooperation 29–31;
    EU-UK relationship 105–9; and Northern
    Ireland 55–6; for peace process 56–60;
    referendum 60–3

Fianna Fáil 13, 33
Foster, Arlene 5, 10, 79, 107
The Fresh Start Agreement 6

Garda Siochána (Irish Police) 72
Garry, J. 62
Givan, Paul 8
Guelke, A. 55–6

Hayward, K. 30, 93, 99
Hillsborough Agreement 5–6
Human Rights Commission 5
Hume, John 21, 22

intergovernmental and civil service cooperation
    23–4; Brexit and 31–6; impact 26–31;
    provisions for 24–6
interim evaluation 4–10
Irish Times 98

Johnson, Boris 108

Lawson, Nigel 76
Lee, Joe 45
Liddle, Roger 74
Lijphart, A. 15, 16
Lynch, Jack 23

MacShane, Denis 80
McCall, C. 31, 98
McCluskey, Conn 85
McDonald, Mary Lou 10
McGuinness, Martin 5–8, 10
Mandelson, Peter 3
Martin, Micheál 7
May, Theresa 8–9, 60, 75, 104
Meehan, Elizabeth 78
Mills, E. 62
Mitchell, George C. 2
Murphy, M. C. 30, 56, 58, 93, 99

Northern Ireland: consociational for 2–3, 13–17; development in 46–7; EU and 55–6, 60–3; governance in 42; nationalism and unionism 85–93
Northern Ireland Act 3
Northern Ireland and Ireland 76
Northern Ireland Economic Strategy 49
Northern Ireland-EU Taskforce (NITF) 59
Northern Irish–Irish civil service cooperation 30
North–South Ministerial Council 27–8
North–South relationship 93–6

The Office of the Northern Ireland Executive (ONIEB) 58
O'Flanagan, Charlie 34
O'Leary, B. 22, 99
Ó Muilleoir, Máirtín 8
O'Neill, Michelle 8, 10

Paisley, Ian 8
Patterson, Owen 4

The PEACE programme 57–8
People Before Profits Alliance (PBPA) 5
Police Service of Northern Ireland (PSNI) 72

Renewable Heating Initiative (RHI) 7
Robinson, Peter 6, 8, 78

Sellars, W. C. 103
Sinn Féin 3, 5–10, 12–13, 32–3
Social Democratic and Labour Party (SDLP) 21, 55
social liberalism 15–16
The Special EU Programmes Body (SEUPB) 29, 58
The St Andrews Agreement 27
The Stormont House Agreement 6, 49–50
The Sunningdale Agreement 23

Tannam, E. 57, 97, 99
Thatcher, Margaret 104
Tiocfaidh ár lá 16
Todd, Jennifer 37
Treaty of Lisbon 79

UKEXIT 9–13
UK-Ireland relations 105
Ulster Unionist Party (UUP) 26, 55
United Kingdom, Brexit bordering 75–6

Walker, G. 97
Walzer, Michael 14

Yeatman, R. 103

For Product Safety Concerns and Information please contact our EU
representative GPSR@taylorandfrancis.com
Taylor & Francis Verlag GmbH, Kaufingerstraße 24, 80331 München, Germany